Park Life

Park Life

The Memoirs of a
Royal Parks Gamekeeper

JOHN BARTRAM

with John Karter

JOHN BLAKE

Published by John Blake Publishing,
The Plaza,
535 Kings Road,
Chelsea Harbour,
London SW10 0SZ

www.johnblakebooks.com

www.facebook.com/johnblakebooks 🄵
twitter.com/jblakebooks 🄴

First published in hardback in 2017
This edition published in 2019

Hardback ISBN: 978 1 78606 279 6
Paperback ISBN: 978 1 78946 105 3
ebook ISBN: 978 1 78606 820 0

British Library Cataloguing-in-Publication Data:

A catalogue record for this book is available from the British Library.

Design by www.envydesign.co.uk

Printed and bound in Great Britain by Clays Ltd, Elcograf S.p.A.

1 3 5 7 9 10 8 6 4 2

John Blake Publishing is an imprint of Bonnier Books UK
www.bonnierbooks.co.uk

For Dave Smith, who made my gamekeeping career possible – a mentor and a friend indeed. And for my wife Maggie, who shared thirty wonderful years of park life with me.

Contents

Foreword

BY

SIR DAVID ATTENBOROUGH

I t is the largest enclosed tract of wild country surrounded by city buildings to be found anywhere in Europe – two and a half thousand acres of woodlands, bracken and open grazing, interspersed with ponds and a brook. This is Richmond Park. Here, five and a half million Londoners and visitors from all over Britain and beyond come every year to enjoy the delights of British wildlife – the ancient oaks, some of which have been standing here for seven centuries, the lumbering flight of stag beetles, those most impressive and weightiest of our nation's insects, the trilling song of soaring skylarks, the enchanting ritualised dances of courting great crested grebes – it is a marvellous vision of wild Britain before humanity overwhelmed so much of it.

Except, of course, that it isn't. It is a carefully and expertly managed community of plants and animals, skilfully controlled by a team including, very crucially, a gamekeeper. That role, for the past thirty years, has been held by John Bartram, the author of this book. It is a difficult task that calls for the detailed understanding of a scientist in managing the wild species in his charge, as well as the tact and persuasion of a diplomat in dealing with the public.

One of the gamekeeper's most difficult tasks concerns the maintenance of the red and fallow deer. There are about six hundred of them, and they are judged by experts to constitute the finest captive herd in this country. But, of course, the ecosystem of which they are a part is far from natural. In earlier times there were wolves that kept the numbers – and the health – of the herd under control. In the seventeenth century, when the wall enclosing the park was first built, the gamekeeper in charge had to ensure that there were stags with fine sets of antlers to reward the king on his hunts. In the twenty-first century, the gamekeeper has to arrange things so that visitors wielding cameras can, instead, get shots of these splendid symbols of the wilderness. How John Bartram managed that task, as well as a multitude of others, he vividly and evocatively describes in the pages that follow.

It is an enthralling story of great interest to anyone – whether one-time visitor or knowledgeable naturalist –

who visits this, one of the country's greatest and most popular natural treasures.

Sir David Attenborough

CHAPTER ONE

A Man for All Seasons

On top of a hill, king of all he surveys, a roaring stag stands silhouetted against the dappled morning sky, sounding out a warning to any rival foolish enough to enter his domain. A formidable presence marking out his territory as the landscape steadily changes face, he has piddled down himself to 'scent' and make his presence felt – and let the hinds know they're on his radar. His autumn coat is a striking shade of reddish brown, but this big stag doesn't just dress to impress: those fearsome-looking antlers are lethal weapons. He's ready and willing to fight to the death, if that's what it takes to see off any challengers. Across the way, in a circle of ancient oak trees with gnarled trunks and twisted boughs that would make the perfect setting for a witches' coven, a group of hinds huddle nervously together; the females of the species, velvety ears twitching, listen out for danger, waiting to see when the stag on the hill will make his move.

For thirty years scenes like this have been the constant background of my working life – a life that seems impossible within the confines of the largest city in Britain. So how did a south London boy find himself in this position: working as the keeper of a large herd of wild deer (and many other wild creatures) in over two thousand acres of unspoilt wild landscape, without ever moving more than a mile or two from his childhood home?

I was born in 1955 in Stretton Road, Ham, where my family still lives. Our house was not much more than a quarter of a mile from the Ham Gate entrance to Richmond Park, which I could never have suspected would be my home and workplace for most of my adult life. Ham then was really a tiny village, without many roads in or out of it. It is set between Richmond and Kingston. From about 1963 onwards, they started to build the big tower blocks that are there now and expand right out to Beaufort Court and Teddington Lock towards Kingston. Before they started this construction, it was open common land with a few empty prefabs from World War Two – a great place to grow up if you liked wildlife.

I was one of nine children: six boys and three girls. None of my brothers or sisters were interested in wildlife as I was, nor did they get involved with it as a job. They could name you birds and animals and liked to see them, but that was as far as it went. My father's love for animals must have put me on the road to liking wildlife of all types, because he was the only member of the family who had animals. I remember as a small child that we had a menagerie of creatures in the back yard; some were there for food and some as pets. We always had dogs, which came off the street. There used to be lots roaming the streets then for some reason and they were never really long-lived as they always picked up something that affected their health when they'd been on the road.

My father took up racing pigeons as a hobby and to act as a food source as well when we were hard up. We also had rabbits and chickens, and they were all destined for the table at some point. Often, my father would kill a couple of pigeons for me and one of my brothers. He always prepared the birds and rabbits for the table and would never let any of us see him killing anything; in fact, half the time we never realised an animal was dead until it was on the plate. I would sometimes feed them and occasionally I would help him clean the pigeon loft.

Because everyone in the village knew of the family's reputation for having all these animals, anybody local who came across an injured or sick wild bird would bring it to my dad to look after. At one time we had a herring gull and also a crow, which landed on the head of one of the lads who lived up our road. It nearly gave him a heart attack as it flew onto him from behind, as he wasn't expecting it. This crow had a bandage round one of its legs where someone had obviously caught it before, treated it and then let it go, so it was semi-tame.

Growing up in Ham during the sixties was great for me and my five brothers as there were so many more open spaces to explore than there are now. If I had my time again, I wouldn't change a thing because it was such a brilliant place to be. It had wildlife – it was a great place for learning what species of animal you were looking at – open fields and Richmond Park. What more could a young boy want?

There used to be pheasants and partridges on Ham Lands, so along with the array of creatures at home I was around animals of some kind every day. I would spend a lot of my time out on the open land around my home and also a lot of time up in Richmond Park. I would be bird nesting – which is illegal now, although I'm not too sure whether it was then – or mousing, which involved lifting boards or bits of timber to see what mice or voles were underneath.

I would also play conkers with my friends, pick blackberries and, of course, go fishing. Many times I would go fishing in Pen Ponds in Richmond Park when the permit was free and covered all parks right up to the Serpentine in Hyde Park – not that I ever got that far. I loved fishing; I really took to it because there was much more to it than just catching fish. It's amazing what wildlife you see when you're sitting still on the river bank. I'm still as avid about it now in my sixties. The River Thames took up a lot of my time. It wasn't like it is today: it had a smell to it and it would be nothing to see dead things floating along. It was a pretty dirty river then – if you fell in you would probably have needed a stomach pump. I remember once there was a die-off and the Mariners Basin at Ham was full of dead fish. This was around 1965 and the smell was unbelievable.

As time went on I hated school and couldn't wait to get out to work. I was better with my hands doing something practical rather than schoolwork. It's funny, I've never been a reader as I always found it boring, and yet here I am writing a book. When I left school I started work at the age of fifteen for Richmond Council as an apprentice blacksmith doing a forty-hour week for £5.10 – the country had just changed to decimal currency in 1971. But after nearly a year I realised it wasn't for me and moved to the parks department as a paper picker. My route was along the Thames to Teddington Lock and back to Richmond. I thought this was great to start with as I could do my birdwatching, see waterfowl on the river and watch any anglers who were fishing there, as by now I was an angling freak – a restful and deeply satisfying hobby I'd carry on throughout my adult life.

It was around this time that the chain of events started that led me to my career in Richmond Park. I got interested in shooting and, when I was eighteen, I bought my first shotgun from a man called Dave Smith, who would go on to become Richmond Park's head gamekeeper and play a very significant role in my life. In the meantime I became an arborist in the tree unit of the parks department, where I stayed for eight years until it reached a point where I was utterly bored with the job and needed to move on. I was thinking about emigrating to Canada with some friends. I had a sister out there and she kept asking when I would be coming out to join her. At this point we didn't know that Esther Rantzen lived in the area. She had a TV programme called *That's Life*, in which – among other things – she highlighted how local councils wasted taxpayers' money. She allegedly complained about the trees in her road, and the council had a knee-jerk reaction, sending us all down there straight away to get on with sorting out the problem.

One day, while we were working on 'Esther's trees', I bumped into an old friend I'd grown up with called Roger Howard, who was tree manager at Kew Gardens. I hadn't seen him for a while, and during the course of our chat, I asked him if any jobs were going at Kew. He said not many, really, just those of labourer, gardener or gamekeeper. I asked him what kind of game they kept at Kew, and he said the gamekeeper's job was to look after the waterfowl collection and the ornamental pheasants and shoot the squirrels and rabbits. I didn't hesitate. I said, 'Please, get me a form. That's what I've always wanted.' I was very nervous on interview day as I didn't know enough about breeding birds, incubation or pest control and was concerned that I would be found out, but in the end I didn't have to worry, as the people interviewing me on the day knew less about the subjects than I did. So I was able to worm my way in and got the job, starting in August 1980. My friends went to Canada and are still out there, married with grown-up kids. I have never regretted not emigrating, though, because I met my wife Maggie and got to live the life of my dreams.

And it hasn't been just my life, but also Maggie's. She has had to work too, part time at Hampton Court, but her main profession has always been as a natural history illustrator – which is how we met. She knew there was a collection of waterfowl at Kew, so she got hold of a guy called Rupert Hastings, and he said, 'It's not me you want to talk to: it's John Bartram, our bird keeper.' So she said, 'How will I find him?' And Rupert replied, 'It won't be difficult: he's the biggest thing in the park!' Goodness knows what she thought, but when we met and got chatting I immediately felt that there was something there. Maggie did a fantastic job of producing a bird pamphlet for Kew, and when I left there to come to Richmond Park, she came with me.

It was at this time that I was introduced to a man called Rodney Woods, through a friend. Rodney bred and kept all sorts of pheasants and chickens on his farm. Well, talk about falling on your feet! Rodney went on to be a great friend and taught me everything I know about pheasants, even down to their various diseases. He was so knowledgeable that he went on to become the top judge for rare breeds in the South East.

One day he allowed me and a friend to go out on his land to do some rabbit control. So there we were, all blacked up and wearing balaclavas, waiting for rabbits to come out in the dead of night, when all of a sudden we heard a pop and saw a flare coming down by parachute. The next thing we knew, there were dozens of men running about with machine guns firing, and shells exploding all around us. We thought World War Three had started. I said to my mate that we'd better get out of there double quick before they thought we were the enemy. In fact, it was the cadets who had come in for a night training session. Talk about wrong place, wrong time!

It was there that I shot my first deer. I came up to Rodney's farm one day and he was skinning a roe buck; I asked him where he found it. He said it had been out in the maize field, and told me that there were lots out there and they were doing all sorts of damage, to the point where the crop would be good only for seed, which fetched a third of the price. I said, 'Why don't you shoot them?' and he said, 'I don't have the time; why don't you do it?' I said, 'I don't have a gun,' and he replied, 'Borrow mine.'

And that's how it all started. I built a high seat up a tree and zeroed his gun, and on my first evening as I sat waiting I could see some bucks creeping out into his field. By the time I had one in my sights I was sure he must have heard my heart pumping, because the adrenaline rush was unbelievable, my chest seemed as if it was going to explode. Having got over that first kill, I shot quite a few deer over the next couple of years and Rodney would sell them on to a dealer.

About this time, when I was working at Kew, a friend said that Dave Smith wanted to see me about ornamental waterfowl and would I go up to his house in Richmond Park, which was the bungalow at Pembroke Lodge, to meet him? Funny how things come back around – it had been a long, long time since Dave and I had spoken. I kept forgetting to go up and, finally, after a year, this friend said Dave was asking after me again and could I get up there? So at last I went and met him, which was the best thing I could have done. Weird how the big finger of fate is pointing at you and you don't realise it at the time. I was on very good terms with Dave when I was at secondary school, but we hadn't met in years. However, like all good friends, we picked up after all that time as if there hadn't been a break. He was after some species of duck for Pegs Pond in Isabella Plantation, which I gave him. After a few months I asked if I could come out on the cull and he asked Michael Baxter Brown, the superintendent, who said yes, I could attend every cull from then on.

Six years later, and fate was at it again. I happened to see an advert for a gamekeeper at Richmond Park in *Shooting Times* and, as luck would have it, the head gamekeeper was – you've guessed it – Dave Smith. I got in touch with Dave and asked him if there would be any point in my applying and he said to go for it. He kept ringing me up to tell me what was happening, and at one point he said there were two hundred applicants from the tip of Scotland, all through Ireland, Wales and England, and that they were being shortlisted down to eight. I thought I wouldn't even get an interview and remarked to Dave that there were men who'd forgotten more than I knew about deer who wouldn't get shortlisted. So what chance did *I* stand? But Dave just kept telling me not to worry, and to go with it – and, to my amazement, I was asked along for an interview.

I realised on the day that all I had to wear was a plum-red jacket with grey slacks. I looked like a Butlin's Redcoat, while all the others were far more suitably attired, so that was unsettling to start with. There were three people doing the interview: Superintendents Michael Baxter Brown (known as 'Brownie') and George Cook, and a lady from Personnel. I knew of Cook, but hadn't met him, and I'd always pictured him short and tubby with a big pointed beard like King Edward VII. It turned out he was six foot six tall, as skinny as a beanpole, with ears that stuck out like ping-pong bats. He started first and asked me, 'You're out shooting rabbits with a two-two rifle and see a deer with a broken leg. Do you think you could shoot him?' I said, 'No, because it's illegal to use a two-two.' Then he said, 'How often do you go to the ranges?' I said, 'Not that often as it's expensive: twenty rounds cost ten pounds.'

I realised he was trying to catch me out, and then he asked me if I would hit the bull before I left the range and if I could get another bullet in the same hole. I replied,

'I'm not John Wayne. I just go to the ranges now and then.' The other two almost fell off their chairs laughing and Cook went a funny shade of red. I got home and was crying into my beer, thinking I'd blown my chance for sure when Dave rang and told me I'd got the job, but to keep quiet until it was in writing.

And so, on 8 August 1986, I became a gamekeeper at Richmond Park. To say I was elated would be the understatement of the century; it meant everything to me. I still can't describe how excited I felt. I'd always thought those gamekeeper jobs would never go to ordinary blokes like me and Dave, who'd been a taxi driver in his previous life. I'd always thought the job would be reserved for men in tweedy suits with handlebar moustaches, who spoke with a plummy accent. I know Dave felt the same way, as did my assistant, Tony Hatton, who is my successor. In a way it meant more to us because we didn't come from a traditional gamekeeper's background. Anyway, the impossible dream came true and the rest, as they say, is history.

The move to Richmond was a big change for Maggie and me. We decided to get married. On the night before our wedding, a great big stag stood on the roundabout at Richmond Gate roaring his head off all night – the one night we wanted some proper sleep to be ready for the marriage ceremony the next day. I ought to have chased the swine off with a broom handle! I might add that no stag has ever done this since. It was as if he knew and was sending us a message of some kind: that some things are just meant to be, perhaps.

Our lodge at Kingston Gate is the gamekeeper's lodge – not that you would think it belonged to one if you walked in. First, I have no antlers on the walls or any stuffed animals, nor do I strut around in a tweed suit. In fact my wife Maggie has an MA in Art and our walls are covered in pictures, photos and prints, which I much prefer. It is quite a normal house really: most gamekeepers I know have similar houses to mine.

However, my lodge does have one thing that many homes may not, and that is a lot of wildlife. One night as an experiment, I tied a dead rabbit to a drainpipe to see if a fox would be bold enough to come close enough to the patio doors to get it. Well, one did turn up and immediately picked up the rabbit and tried to run off, nearly pulling my drainpipe off the wall and almost causing him to lose all his gnashers. He did this two or three times, but then became so angry that at one point he was jumping on the rabbit in frustration. After an hour or so of pure determination, he got it free. It was a bit of a tease for him but highly diverting watching him trying so hard to get his dinner.

Another time, I had three grass snakes all coiled up on my patio sunning themselves. We always had grass snakes because they bred in my compost heap every year for twenty years – a constant supply. Then there were the stag beetles that would go on the wing trying to find a mate: great big lumbering things with no idea of where they were going. I always had timber edges to my garden, so there was a place for them to lay eggs and carry on the species. I also had mortar bees that made their home in my brickwork outside my back door. I didn't even realise such things existed until they made holes in the mortar and then, I presume, laid their eggs and built a sealed entrance. It is an amazing garden.

So, from my earliest years as a child in Ham, I have been surrounded by animals – wild and domestic. I have been very lucky. How many children growing up in south London today would have those opportunities? The world has changed too much. Now that this chapter of my life is coming to an end, one of the things that concerns me about moving out of Kingston Gate Lodge is how I'll cope with neighbours. The only neighbours I've had for the past thirty years have been badgers, foxes and deer.

I've worked closely with, and been fortunate to meet, some amazing people during my time in the park. The memories I'll take with me will be as varied as the situations I've found myself in over the years. And, believe me, I've had to deal with just about every possible scenario you could imagine – and a few you couldn't – as you will see.

CHAPTER TWO

The Jewel in
the Crown

Richmond Park is unique – the jewel in the Royal Parks crown. 2,360 acres in extent, it is a Site of Special Scientific Interest and a National Nature Reserve, embedded in a great metropolis. It is home to a combined six hundred red and fallow deer and many other creatures. And it has been my habitat as well – for thirty years. It is the largest Royal Park, and the largest enclosed tract of wild country surrounded by city to be found anywhere in Europe – a true oasis in the capital.

During the rutting season the deer are the obvious focus of attention for everyone who comes through the gates, but the park itself is equally hypnotic in its own way. Across the broad sweep of the grassland, the autumn colours are stunning, painting the trees in every shade of brown, gold and orange that the mind's eye could imagine. As black-headed gulls shriek overhead, leaves and acorns are tumbling down from the trees, forming a deep-pile carpet that scrunches underfoot. A pair of bob-tailed rabbits, dead ringers for Fiver and Bigwig from *Watership Down*, skip lightly across the carpet, pausing now and then to gather a morsel or glance anxiously around, before scuttling off into the sanctuary of the undergrowth. High above, a sinister shape among the scudding clouds, a kestrel hovers menacingly, its eyes like laser beams, ready to arrow down mercilessly on its prey.

This is a snapshot of my working environment. Imagine going to work to be greeted by this scene. I am eight miles from the centre of London, with St Paul's Cathedral looming in the distance among the sprawl of office blocks. Cars pass by in steady streams as the rush hour reaches its peak, but this is as different from commuting as Mars is from Marble Arch.

This is nature at its most compelling, in a setting steeped in history. Richmond Park – once a royal hunting ground, and home to earls, countesses, prime ministers, a princess, a president and a film star – is a magnificent beast of a park at any time, but arguably puts on its most spectacular suit of clothes as the year enters its final quarter, making it more than ever a magnet for deer lovers, birdwatchers, butterfly and beetle buffs, television crews, professional photographers and amateur snappers.

From a childhood spent only a quarter of a mile from the park, I can remember all the gamekeepers right back to one called Mr Wonham. I remember seeing him riding his bike many times with a length of baler twine tied around the middle of his coat. After him I knew all the other keepers quite well, especially one called Buster Brown, whom I classified as a mate. We fished and played in a darts team together, and I was always up at his lodge, often to babysit so he and his wife could go out. Following him were Bill Joyce, Dave Smith, me and then Kia Handley and Tony Hatton. I think I'm the longest-serving gamekeeper since Mr Wonham, who came after the war and left in the early seventies. I make that twenty-five years he served, whereas all the others went before completing twenty. And I will have done thirty when I leave.

Richmond Park was a quiet park when I was a child, with sheep all over the place. It was like being out in the countryside. The sheep used to sleep in the road at night as it kept its warmth from the day, so people really had to be careful driving through at last knockings. Buster Brown told me he hardly ever had to be called out to deal with deer or the two hundred sheep when they were in here. I think there were even cattle roaming free back in the forties and fifties, which really shows just how little the park was used by the public. What a difference compared with today's 5.5 million visitors who pass through the gates annually.

In my early days, the park was hardly used, and we could do our shooting until 10 a.m. or sometimes 11 a.m. You wouldn't usually meet a soul. But one day Dave and I were shooting up the Queen's Ride and a woman appeared and complained that shooting at that time of the morning was dangerous, so Brownie, the superintendent, said that in future we should stop at 9 a.m. It turned out that this woman was the wife of Sir Kenneth Newman, the Commissioner of Police, and when Dave found out, he was mightily relieved that he'd restrained himself and hadn't told her to buzz off! That happened four or five years into the job – and considering how many dog walkers, cyclists and general visitors use the park at all times nowadays, it's a necessary requirement.

I've been in love with Richmond Park for as long as I've known it. If you asked me why, I'd say, 'How long have you got?' It's a unique place, in so many different ways. It offers something for everyone, whether they are first-timers or 'hardy annuals', which is why its popularity continues to soar, as the ever-increasing number of visitors indicates. You could, for example, take tea on the terrace at Pembroke Lodge, a beautiful eighteenth-century house steeped in history, which is located at the highest point in the park and offers stunning views over the Thames Valley to the west – you can see Windsor Castle on a clear day. Pembroke Lodge is a popular venue for marriage celebrations, so do not be surprised if you see a bride and groom in full wedding gear crossing your path during your visit.

You might follow this with a stroll through the veteran oak trees of Sidmouth Wood and Queen Elizabeth's Plantation, some of which are between five and seven hundred years old, to view the waterfowl freely on show in and around Pen Ponds; or a meander through Isabella Plantation, savouring the incredibly rich mix of flora and fauna, alongside the gorgeous water features; or simply a walk across any area of the park to enjoy spectacular scenery, with herds of red and fallow deer running wild.

For those who enjoy architecture, there are many fine buildings apart from Pembroke Lodge, including White Lodge, where Nelson sketched out his battle plans for Trafalgar in red wine during a dinner in 1805, and which is now home to the Royal Ballet School; and Thatched House Lodge, an eighteenth-century mansion used by Britain's first prime minister, Sir Robert Walpole – and, it is believed, King George II, as a hunting lodge – and which is now the private home of Princess Alexandra.

The history of the park dates back to 1637, when King Charles I, who was 'excessively affected to Hunting, and the Sports of the Field', having bought off local landowners and ridden roughshod over others, completed the enclosure of the area we now know as Richmond Park by the construction of a perimeter wall. The wall was actually built without foundations and had to be repaired time and again. The older sections that are still in place are thought to date back to the mid-eighteenth century. Much of it is now classed as a Grade II listed structure.

Various stories are told about monarchs and their

connections with the park, some true, others not. It was said that Henry VIII waited on the mound that now bears his name – and offers a fabulous view across London to St Paul's Cathedral – for a signal that Anne Boleyn had been executed at the Tower of London in 1536. Actually, he was miles away hunting on that day. What is true is that George III used to shoot turkeys in the park, and Queen Elizabeth, the Queen Mother, lived at White Lodge in the park with her husband King George VI in 1923–24. Marshall Tito of Yugoslavia also stayed at White Lodge during a state visit to Britain in 1955.

You can also find remnants of medieval features in the park. In the northern section there is a line of oaks to the west of Holly Lodge that marked a medieval field boundary. There is also a path in Barn Wood next to the fence of Two Storm Wood that was once a medieval lane running from Mortlake to Ham, and to the west of that path there are traces of ridge and furrow ploughing. I wish someone could invent a time machine so that I could go back to Henry VIII's day and see what the park looked like then as opposed to now. The place truly drips in its rich history and heritage.

This is what makes Richmond Park such an interesting place: so much has gone on here over the centuries, far more than in any other park. During World War One, there was a military hospital located between Bishop's Pond and Conduit Wood for all the injured coming back from France. Around fifty South African soldiers died there and are buried in Richmond Cemetery. In World War Two, the military took over 90 per cent of the park for the war effort. My father did some of his military training here, he told me, especially night manoeuvres.

There also used to be a Victorian-style bandstand just inside the gate as you came in. I can remember coming up with my mum to sit and listen to the band playing on a Sunday. The bandstand was eventually moved to Regent's Park in London in 1975, where, in July 1982, the IRA detonated a bomb underneath it, killing seven men of the Royal Green Jackets. When you read diaries from the records office, they say things such as, 'Not so many hares this year; too many dogs' (hares were still here up until the 1960s), and, 'Couldn't count the deer this year because the undergrowth has come up so high we can't see them.'

I read some diaries years ago that came from the Public Records Office at Kew, and in one of them there was a brief note to say that a member of staff had gone up and over Spankers Hill to see if the cattle were OK, and he was walking through six inches of snow. And this was in June. The year was 1956, and at that time Richmond had cattle roaming free across the park as well as sheep, and probably over a thousand deer as well. It's amazing that there was anything green left with that many grazers. I suppose it was a way of making an income and keeping the grass levels down across the park, but also you have to remember that the park wasn't under pressure from the public as it is today, so these animals could roam free.

Now fast-forward to 2000, when Richmond Park was given National Nature Reserve status. Having that title means we have to be seen to enhance our environment and habitat to increase things such as acid grassland, which is one of the things we were given the status for in the first place. Natural England told us we were undergrazed and needed to sort it out and try to increase it if possible. They suggested using cattle, not sheep, as sheep tend to crop everything down to a billiard-table level, which is the total opposite of what we want.

The deer have helped towards creating acid grassland over the centuries, but they really aren't the best animals to do this, as they are fussy herbivores and nibble rather than completely graze. Cows, on the other hand, are perfect, and in 2008 it was decided we would borrow some hardy cattle and to pen them in an enclosure of four hectares just outside the yard at Holly Lodge. These particular cattle were two head of white Gloucester borrowed from Hounslow Council Trust, hardy sorts because they were going to be in there from January to May in all weathers through a winter–spring grazing project. The following year we borrowed three cows. We did it slowly to begin with to see how the cattle would fare. Later on we borrowed more cattle from the Surrey Wildlife Trust and started to bring them in earlier in the year, in October, because it was felt a winter graze would be best. We were told that this was the best time and that these were the kinds of animals that were needed to do the job.

At the time, I had Kia Handley working with me and we had to go on a course to learn about dealing with cattle. When we completed the course we were certificated for cattle management, which was necessary, as these animals were going to be our responsibility once they arrived here and would need to be screened every day to see they were OK. So the pen area was worked out and put up, we got in drinking troughs and electric fencing, and the cows were put in. It was fascinating watching the deer on the outside looking at the cows as if to say, 'What the hell are they? They don't look like deer or smell like them.' They were really taken aback when the cows first came.

The first year went by and the cows were returned to their owners. Later in the summer our ecology team went in to see what sorts of plant life had changed, if any, and to establish whether the project was going to be a success. It turned out that cows do two things that help us with acid grassland. First, they are naturally a heavy animal and bruise the rhizomes of bracken, helping to kill it. This is important because it slowly covers all of the park and needs controlling. Second, when they eat, they pull up a fair mouthful with a bit of soil attached. This creates a little shallow hole, which apparently is the ideal for perfect acid grassland. They are also good at composting. These results showed that the project was a good idea and it was decided that we should continue with it.

We've progressed since then, and by year eight (2016) were talking about getting in more animals – fifteen to twenty of them. And, rather than a conventional fence, we would use an underground electric fence, which would cover a bigger area, and the cows would wear a collar that would give them a small shock if they got too close to the fence line. It sounds cruel but it isn't. Unlike humans, animals are quick to learn from their mistakes. So, if they get too near the underground fence, the collar starts bleeping and if they continue the bleep gets faster to let them know they will receive a jolt. Apparently, they pick this up very quickly and get to know their area, Also, without a fence, it looks a bit more natural.

This is to be the next project regarding the cows at Richmond Park. When this all takes place, I will no longer be here, so I won't have anything to do with it. On a happier note, one year we borrowed our cattle and, during the period we kept them, one of them gave birth to a calf, a little boy, which was kind of nice. The owners weren't aware that she was pregnant. Even though they occasionally showed up to look at the cows, they still didn't realise that she was going to give birth, so she caught us all on the hop.

I shall have some happy memories of the cattle, especially times when we had a bit too much snow. I would take a bale of hay up there for them to eat and on a couple of occasions they got so excited at seeing this bale when I called them that they charged at me. Imagine Highland cows with massive horns thundering towards you – not something you'd deliberately encourage. But, as luck would have it, they stopped about six feet in front of me. I don't mind admitting that I was worried at the time, with one-ton cows charging towards me in the middle of an open field and nowhere to go. It's a shame we can't leave the animals to roam freely across the park and do their own thing. Can you visualise rare breed cows such as longhorns running free? It would be lovely to see but, alas, with so many people here now and with dogs all wanting their bit of space, all of which is slowly increasing, it just wouldn't be fair on a large, slow-moving creature like a cow to be caught out by a dog chasing the living daylights out of it.

As well as being an incredible site of natural and historical interest, Richmond Park is also a hardy, venerable old place which has seen some adventures – and some misadventures. It takes something out of the ordinary to force the park to close. Sometimes big events such as the Olympics in 2012, and other cycling and running races, will mean that public access is restricted. And I recall only too well how in February 2001 the park had to be shut for a far more sinister reason. A serious outbreak of foot-and-mouth disease across the UK forced the park to close its gates to the public for seven weeks. The only people who were allowed access were essential staff and residents such as Princess Alexandra, as well as four hundred pupils of the Royal Ballet School in White Lodge.

It was an extremely worrying time for us because farmers all over England were destroying their herds and burning the carcasses. You were forbidden to transport animals and even horse race meetings were cancelled. Sheep farmers who had, say, a thousand animals ready for slaughter had to hang onto them and, to make matters worse, they had to go through the winter period and keep them without any food. They would usually have been in the shops and the farmers would have been getting income from them, so they were hit badly. It was all very well those people in suits in offices making sweeping statements, but they didn't stop to think about the impact it had on the poor farmers.

As far as we were concerned, you never knew if and when it would come into the park, because you couldn't stop foxes and squirrels and other animals coming over the walls. There was talk that, if it did arrive in the park, we would have to get in a team of men with guns to shoot everything they saw. Then we would have to dig a huge trench out on the Flying Field and have a mass cremation. We had numerous meetings with DEFRA and our vet, Michael Simons, and the consensus was that there would be no option but to shoot the entire deer herd.

I was thinking that if that really happened there would be no reason for me to be here. I had visions of the management saying that now the herd had gone they wouldn't bother replacing them. We were out there every second of the day, watching the herd, looking for signs of foot-and-mouth, which include salivating, blistered mouths, swollen glands, things like that. People used to ask if the animals would die anyway if they weren't destroyed. During the outbreak in 2001, there were rumours that French farmers were apparently shutting their cattle up in barns and leaving them there because the disease can manifest just like flu symptoms and the animals would eventually get over it. However, the official line is that, while the disease does not typically kill the animals, it inhibits their ability to eat in the short term and permanently affects their health, productivity and overall wellbeing, so that is why it's considered necessary to destroy infected animals to prevent more getting sick.

In order to protect the animals from the disease, all those entering were forced to undergo a strict disinfectant procedure. And the animals soon cottoned on to what was happening. They began doing things they wouldn't usually do and showing up in places where you'd never usually see them, as I can testify personally, because I had a load of them hanging around outside my house near Kingston Gate. I came home one day at about midday and there was a large herd of hinds all around Kingston Gate and in the road. Usually at that time of day, they would move into the park itself because of people and cars coming in.

Other animals took advantage of the closure. One day, a moorhen flew into my garden and stayed on my pond for a day. God knows why and where it came from, because the nearest pond to me was Gallows pond, which was dry at that time. I also had foxes walking around my garden at all times of night and day and even had a beautiful cock pheasant fly over my garage roof before landing in my garden and staying for a couple of days. It was as if all the wildlife knew that the park was shut to everyone and they could all go wherever they pleased.

My assistant, Kia, and I had a great time – if only we could shut every six months. We could walk anywhere with a gun and not be bothered by anyone, which meant we could go into places that would usually have been full of people. And for once we collected every cast antler, which showed just how many the public find and take home, because in the normal course of events we're lucky to find six. We were brought back to reality by Tony Blair, who was prime minister at the time. He forced us to reopen because it was coming up to Easter, saying, 'I want you open for Good Friday regardless'. This decision seemed ridiculous in view of the serious nature of the threat. Luckily, the park managed to escape the disease; somehow we got away with it.

There is one other thing that has managed to shut the park, to traffic at least: snow. If it's going to snow it usually happens around February time, and I have known at least one period when you couldn't see the posts on the side of the road, which are a foot tall. It was difficult to determine what was road and what wasn't, so we had to ban all traffic for two or three days.

A winter like that makes spring all the more welcome. This is a lovely time of year, with all the flowers showing across the park, and a starting time of 5.30 a.m. seems not quite as bad as it does during winter. If plants and flowers are your thing, there is no better place to be than Isabella Plantation, where you will see beautiful evergreen azaleas lining the ponds and streams, reaching their peak of flowering in late April and early May. (There are about thirty ponds in the park. Some – including Barn Wood Pond, Bishop's Pond, Gallows Pond, Leg of Mutton Pond, Martin's Pond and White Ash Pond – have been created to drain the land or to provide water for livestock. The Pen Ponds, which in the past were used to rear carp for food, date from 1746.) You'll also find species of rhododendron, camellia and magnolia, as well as the exotic-looking, bright yellow skunk cabbage.

Indeed, when people think of Richmond Park they inevitably think of the deer, but it's also renowned for the incredible variety of plant life, most notably the trees. The park's trees are one of its most attractive features, enhancing the landscape throughout the seasons in an often spectacular way. As Adam Curtis, one of the park's senior management team, wrote in the Friends of Richmond Park's *Guide to Richmond Park*, 'They define the landscape's character, filtering out the presence of London'.

There are around a hundred and thirty thousand

trees scattered across the woodlands and parkland. This 'natural' landscape has in fact been created over a thousand years of active management, which has put in place a mixture of features superimposed on each other. This has created a rich and varied treescape distributed over many different areas, including, but not limited to, open parkland, which consists mostly of grass with relatively few trees; unenclosed woodlands, which are densely planted; enclosed woodlands, which are fenced off from the deer and have more ground flora and trees below six feet; riparian woodlands, which contain species specialised to grow on wet ground; and scrub enclosures, small areas of low dense hawthorn or gorse cover.

In percentage terms, 45 per cent of the park's trees are oak, 20 per cent are beech, and another 20 per cent is made up of hawthorn, birch and hornbeam: 10 per cent is a variety of indigenous and exotic species, from willows and alders to eighteenth century cedars and twentieth century sugar maples; and the remaining 5 per cent is sweet and horse chestnut.

If only trees could talk, they could tell some stories. Our veteran oaks, some of which are between five and seven hundred years old, are a particular draw, predating the enclosure of the park, in 1637, by Charles I. Behind the yard in Holly Lodge is a trail that has been there for five hundred years, with six original oak trees still alive and in place along its edge, including one veteran oak which was pollarded hundreds of years ago to accommodate the three thousand turkeys that used to roam the park.

(The birds were for hunting purposes, and pollarding the trees allowed the birds to get up to roost at night away from the predators, including King George III, who apparently used to have them flushed out by dogs and then shoot them when they tried to find sanctuary up in the branches.)

The trees are also a big part of the deer diet. Although they do consume grass, deer prefer to browse rather than graze, so they create what's known as a 'browse-line', where they've munched away at low-hanging branches. When the great storm of 1987 hit the park, the browse-line became more of a floor-line as trees tumbled over like dominoes. The memory of the sheer devastation that confronted me afterwards comes flooding back every time autumn rolls around. In fact, it's difficult not to be reminded of that extraordinary night because there are still fallen trees lying around in various stages of decay all over the park.

It has also been said that the park contains a magical healing tree. It did once have a 'shrew ash', which was said to have healing properties. Apparently, they used to place a live shrew in a hole in the trunk of the tree, and then fill it in, which people believed conjured up magic. Mothers would pass their sick children through a cleft in the tree, and it was said that this healed them. This practice went on from medieval times until, it is believed, the nineteenth century. Although he couldn't recall when he had last seen the shrew ash in use, a writer in the *Mid-Surrey Times* of 1874 claimed that it was still used and believed in then. The remains of the ancient tree finally collapsed in the great storm of 1987.

But the storm was not the only thing which has changed the treescape here dramatically. Back in the seventies, when I worked for Richmond Council, Dutch elm disease broke out, killing thousands of elm trees. Elm trees were brought into the UK and used for timber, but they still had the bark on and underneath the bark were loads of beetles. We haven't got any elm trees left in Richmond Park; they all had to be cut down. There was a huge mass of elms by Ham Gate at one point, but they all had to be chopped down because of Dutch elm disease.

Because of the amount of ancient timber, the Park is remarkable for the insect life and fungi associated with old trees. But it also has a diverse wildlife of smaller creatures, including woodpeckers, squirrels, rabbits, snakes, frogs, toads, stag beetles and many other insects and varieties of fungi. It is particularly notable for its rare beetles. And in recent years the Park has been invaded by large numbers of ring-necked parakeets, which have bred from birds that escaped from captivity. Who knows which species could land in this verdant breeding ground next?

And that's just a brief account of this wonderful place. Small wonder I fell in love with it.

CHAPTER THREE

The Great Storm

The great storm of 1987 is in itself an indelible piece of the park's history, and deserves its story to be told within these pages. On the night of 15 October, a storm of hurricane velocity swept across south east England, with a highest recorded gust of 130 mph. It fell at a time when the trees were still in leaf and, furthermore, heavy with rain. The damage was indescribable. An estimated 15 million trees were lost nationwide. The ancient timber of Richmond Park was devastated.

The storm happened just over a year after I first started in the job. I was actually on holiday in Cornwall the night it took place, and we were in its eye, so we didn't even feel a puff of wind. I remember reading about the chaos across the whole of Surrey after the most damaging storm for 284 years. Hurricane-force winds suddenly whipped up seemingly out of nowhere, shortly after midnight, and one and a half million trees came crashing down across the county in six hours.

When I walked out into the park on my return, the scene that greeted me was unbelievable – it was as if the atomic bomb had been dropped and the shock wave had flattened everything. Fifteen hundred trees came down in Sidmouth Wood alone. With many of the trees being so old, you might have expected that they would be deep-rooted and able to withstand the wind better. But, as it happens, Richmond Park stands on a shallow layer of topsoil above a vast bed of hoggin, which is a mixture of sand and gravel, the kind of thing builders call 'hardcore', so most of the trees are shallow-rooted. As they crashed down with tremendous force, fences were smashed everywhere, so the deer could come and go as they pleased within the park.

More significantly, there were seven breaches of the perimeter wall, which allowed fourteen bucks to escape and roam all over the neighbourhood. They caused mayhem among the locals, setting up temporary homes everywhere from cemeteries to back gardens to Richmond Station. And you had to wait until someone rang in about one; you couldn't just go charging round the streets with a gun. As soon as they'd rung in, I needed to phone up to get a police officer to accompany me because, as soon as you left the park, you were in different zones, which the police needed to be updated about so they knew where we were. So the officer might say, 'I'm in Zone GH now, but the deer's moved on, so we're entering Zone AC now.'

The one who ended up at the station led me a merry dance. I chased him from garden to garden and he eventually got up on the railway. The last time I saw him he was heading down a tunnel leading to the underground station. We never found out what happened to him. I reckon he must have been hit by a train or blown up when he stood on the live rail. It took weeks and weeks to track them all down. We got four or five quickly back to the park alive and safe, but the rest had to be shot. You've got to remember that the poor old deer are well out of their comfort zone running round in the streets. They're not used to it. And you couldn't tranquillise them because, if you missed and someone picked up the immobilising dart, it would kill them.

I reckon I aged twenty years during those weeks after the storm, because it's nerve-racking running round the local streets with a gun in your hand, with people shouting all sorts of things at you. The problem is that, even if you find the deer, you can't just shoot them there and then unless you have a proper backdrop, meaning that if you miss with your shot the bullet won't be at risk of injuring someone – or worse. It needs to land somewhere safe. Many times I've had a deer lined up for a shot, but I couldn't take it because he had nothing behind him and the bullet could have just flown off and hit someone. I had to wait until he moved on and then follow him until he had a tree or a wall behind him, where the bullet could lodge safely. The armed divisions of the police get specialist training for that kind of thing, but we had nothing at all, so it was really a case of learning by experience.

That chaotic episode after the storm brings to mind the time when a woman from the Civil Service's Human Resources department came to see me for a job evaluation. One question I had to answer was whether I considered my decision-making to be 'not significant', 'moderately significant', or 'significant'. When I ticked the box marked 'significant' she had a go at me, saying, 'How can you tick "significant" when people in far higher positions than you don't say that?' I said, 'Well, let me give you an example. If I'm called out for a deer that's escaped and it's running wild in the local high street, I have to weigh up the risk of trying to shoot it, because if I miss I might take out three old ladies in Sainsbury's. I'd say that's pretty damned significant, wouldn't you?'

I certainly proved my point and blew them all away. My colleagues were all arguing the toss, saying, 'Leave it in'; 'Take it out'; 'He's right'; 'No, he's not'; and so on. It was hilarious. The following week we received a letter saying that on no account could we go outside the park with a firearm. Nowadays any deer that escape from the park are taken care of by the police; we don't get involved at all. Legally, no one owns a deer until it dies on their land, the exceptions being Richmond Park, where they are owned by the Queen, and on a farm where they're tame and are bucket-fed and ear-tagged. We ear-tag ours for ageing, not traceability, and the farm-raised ones have passports, whereas ours don't.

Over the years, we've had deer getting out all over the place. Possibly the worst one we had to deal with was on the Roehampton estate, which is a cluster of tower blocks at one edge of the park. A buck got into the underground car park and was running amok. Dave, the head keeper, actually did the shooting and he asked me to video it. You should have seen the stress showing on Dave's face – he was ashen.

There were further losses in the Burns' Day storm of 1990. Subsequent replanting included a new plantation, Two Storm Wood, a short distance into the park from Sheen Gate. Some extremely old trees that survived can also be seen inside this enclosure, fitting monuments to that most turbulent of nights.

CHAPTER FOUR

A Year with the Deer

I've never tried to bluff my way in life. If you try to bluff your way through, it has a habit of coming back and biting you later on. I've always wanted to find out exactly what's required in terms of doing a job and I've never been afraid to approach someone who knows a lot about a particular subject and ask them to share their knowledge. That said, when I started the Richmond job, I never felt out of my depth because I was shadowing Dave for a number of years and I'd also been out in the park volunteering at weekends, learning the work.

The bulk of that work, my work, here in Richmond Park, has been managing the deer herd. With no natural predators to control their numbers, deer will proliferate, graze the environment flat, and eventually decline in quality and numbers, doing much damage on the way.

In effect I have been Mr Big Predator in the Park for thirty years – but with this crucial difference: I and other keepers are big predators who can foresee the results of their predation and plan accordingly. Without wishing to sound arrogant, as far as the deer herd is concerned, we've set the bar so high that experts in the field are amazed by what they find here. The answer is that our magnificent herd is made possible by the meticulously planned year that we keep to here at the park – a year which takes us from season to season, from rut to calving and beyond, each phase bringing its own unique magic.

THE RUT

People ask me what my favourite time of year is, which is an unfair question because every month brings something special with it. However, I must admit that if I was pressed to choose which my favourite season, I would have to plump for autumn. Autumn is when the park is at its most stunning and it's showtime for the deer. I'm clearly not alone in this, because the park draws hordes of visitors from all over the world through its gates at this time, with many of them coming here specifically for the deer rut. As the landscape's changing face heralds the passing of the year, the age-old ritual of the rut is reaching its peak. The clash of antlers and the roaring of the stags as these magnificent creatures fight for the right to mate symbolises the park's universal appeal. Yet the image of two stags with their antlers locked together offers only a small part of the overall picture, and there are many aspects of this fascinating breeding ritual that remain hidden to the casual observer.

For anyone who has never sat and watched red deer rut, it really is an exciting thing to do and should be on your bucket list. You really are seeing Mother Nature in the raw, and it's very primitive. When two big stags are going at it, it's amazing to witness the power they have. I've had them chase the Land Rover many times because they feel threatened, and they have punctured the tyres. You get to see all the body messages being sent without uttering a sound, just through simple posture and movement. If only humans could do the same, wouldn't life be different?

In contrast to the roaring sound made by stags (adult male red deer), bucks (male fallow) produce a loud burp as a way of frightening off rivals and avoiding a fight. There's scientific evidence to show that the deeper the belch, the more the other bucks will walk away because they feel threatened. The young ones will be hanging around all day long like flies round a cow's backside waiting for their chance. If two older males are fighting each other the youngsters will charge in and split the females up. They all cop the odd girl to have their wicked way with, but in general it's the master stags who run the show.

Contrary to their popular image, stags will fight only if it's absolutely necessary. Unlike many humans, they're not innately aggressive, and if they resort to brute force, it's invariably as a response to a threat of one kind or another. And they wouldn't attack a human unless they felt threatened, although they do respond when people take liberties. This is usually because people don't appreciate that deer are wild animals, which in practical terms means that they're unpredictable. They're not fed out of a bucket and they don't like being handled. Just because they're contained within the walls of the park, it doesn't mean they're any less wild. I always emphasise that point and tell people to take great care.

In the rutting season, male deer are forced into defensive action when a rival arrives on the scene seeking to deprive them of the harem of around thirty females they've carefully accumulated. Ideally, what they'd like to do is just keep hold of their harem, and if they never saw another stag, they'd be in their element, because they'd be rutting night and day. The females don't all come into season at the same time, but a stag knows when one does and then he'll service her. Like most boys with their hormones running wild, if they can get a female without having a punch-up, that suits them fine.

What happens in reality is usually very different, however. The stag has a piece of territory that's known as his 'stand' and what you don't see is the invisible line around it where he's scented. When another stag comes across that line, it's inevitable that he's got to fight if he wants to keep those hinds on that stand. Otherwise, he'll be ousted and he'll have to find somewhere else in the park to acquire a stand in the hope that the hinds are going to come his way. That means he might have to challenge another stag around the corner and try to get *his* stand.

They do fight to the death sometimes, but they're not doing it deliberately. You've got to appreciate that when you've got two huge master stags, weighing up to a quarter of a ton, pushing against one another, the power they generate is huge. One might back up a bit because he's losing, and turn sideways just enough so one of his rival's tines (row of antlers) will go through his ribs. As I said, they're definitely not setting out to kill. I had a young buck running around the park once going crazy, bashing into everything. He'd lost both his eyes in a fight and he ran into the middle of Leg of Mutton Pond because he didn't know what else to do. He felt water on his legs and I suppose he felt safe. We were able to shoot him in the middle of the pond, which was the kindest thing to do.

The young ones do play-fight, but they're not really fighting: they're just messing about. They're getting used to their antlers and what it feels like to have a tussle. Sometimes you get a third one coming along and he wants to join in – typical kids! So you've got three heads together and then a fourth one joins in and he might stab one in the side – he doesn't mean to kill him, but he'll go in sideways and go straight through the chest and lungs. I've seen loads killed like that. They just don't realise the consequences of what they're doing. It's all part of the learning process and growing up.

When they do fight they can get into all kinds of trouble

they hadn't bargained for, which often means I have to come along and try to sort it out. For example, we had a stag from Gunton Park in Norfolk for six or seven years, and he was at the top of the breeding pack. In his last year we discovered he had a cataract in one eye and we'd already decided we were going to take him out during the cull in February. Anyway, he decided he was going to have fisticuffs with another stag during the rut, and the pair were literally locked together.

I said to my assistant, Kia, if it's that bad I'll shoot the big one with the cataract because we're going have to do that anyway, and leave the other one. Usually when you do that the one you've shot drops to the floor and the other one can pull away, but when we got up close we found that the big old Norfolk boy had put his antler into the other one's mouth and smashed all his teeth out. So now I was thinking that I'd have to shoot them both because one's got a cataract and the other's got no teeth.

Kia went back to get the gun and I got hold of this big plank of wood and was swinging on it trying to get them apart. I was on the side of the Land Rover so that if they attacked I could get away quickly, but despite all my efforts, they stayed locked. Kia came back with the gun and I told him to shoot the one that had all the teeth missing because, although the Norfolk stag had a cataract, he could walk away all right. So we shot the one with the missing teeth thinking that, as it dropped, the other would break free, but it didn't – they were still stuck together. We ended up shooting them both and we had a devil of a job getting them apart; their antlers were well and truly locked together.

The rut carries on until November, although the females don't all come into season at the same time. Ideally, you'd want them all to conceive at the same time and all give birth on the same day. But that's like winning the lottery: it's not going to happen. The real problem is late-born calves, which are the result of young stags who've been waiting for their chance to pick up a hind when the rut is over. Around December time when the master stags have gone off to lick their wounds and recover from their exertions, a young stag might find a hind who has come into season late and get her pregnant.

Ideally, you don't want calves born at the end of the year. You'd like them born in May or June when it's warm, there's plenty of plant growth and the best food is available, so the mothers eat well and produce good milk full of nutrients. In the winter months the grass has stopped growing – when the frost hits deer depend on supplementary food, which we give them seven days a week. A late-born calf never makes a good animal because it hasn't had the benefit of proper nutrition. When I've carried out the first stage of the cull, in November, I've sometimes had to shoot a mother as well as her young because, if she's late once, she's always late. She'll never give birth with the rest of the girls in May and June.

After the rut is finally finished, in December, the stags must take time out to recover from their amorous exertions, which means trying to recover on sleep, putting their body fat back on and going off to lick their wounds, which they've sustained from fighting rivals. Their wounds often become infected and cause abscesses, and it doesn't help that a stag's coat is like an eco-system all of its own with spiders and all kinds of creepy-crawlies running around inside it. Deer's outer hairs are known as 'pins' and each hair is hollow – that's why fishermen use them to make their fly lures. The inner hair is like grey wool.

If you see a big stag before the rut in September, he looks like a hippo with a huge fat belly on him that goes right round from his shoulders to his back legs. You see that same animal in late October during the rut and his belly will have flattened right out. It just shrinks like a balloon that's had the air let out of it. If you opened up that animal before the rut you'd find that the fat wall down its spine would just be thick white layers of creamy fat. But after the rut it's so thin that it looks like tracing paper; there's not one strand of fat anywhere. If you held it up to the light you would be able to see right through it.

And now the poor animal has not only picked up injuries from fighting as well as rutting, but his sleep deprivation is vast. When you see these big old males and they've had a real hard time of it, they're so exhausted that they're asleep on their legs. And you often see them completely out for the count.

Having used up all their energy and all their fat reserves, the worst is still to come: they've got to try to get through the winter – the toughest part of the year when there's next to no food – with no body fat. That's why we do the supplementary feeding – it's mainly for the stags and bucks. It's a hard life if you're a male deer. A lot of people think they're lazy for lying around all summer getting fat, but there's a reason for it. Mind you, everything's relative, and, compared with other deer habitats – such as Scotland, where it can be bitterly cold and food is desperately hard to come by – Richmond Park is like the Garden of Eden for these boys.

TO CULL OR NOT TO CULL?

People question the need to cull the Richmond deer. But it's a necessity, and the only real questions are: when, how, and how many?

We cull the deer purely to maintain the wellbeing of the herd by keeping the number in balance with the environment and available food supplies, as well as looking after the ecology of the park. If you just left them alone they'd continue producing more and more young and there would be nothing green left in the park for them to eat. They'd be starving, emaciated and diseased, and a lot of them would end up with serious deformities. The question you've got to ask yourself is: 'Do we want a park like that?'

Simon Richards, superintendent for Richmond Park, put out a comprehensive statement on behalf of the

Royal Parks in December 2009 in order to explain the need to cull the deer. The text was agreed following consultation between the Royal Parks, the British Deer Society and the Deer Initiative, who are regarded as the main organisations dealing with the welfare and management of deer nationally. In a nutshell, Simon's statement explained why keeping deer numbers at sustainable levels is vital for their own welfare. Humanely shooting deer to achieve that goal is approved by both the BDS and the DI. They agree that culling is essential in order to avoid the problems of disease, malnutrition and damage to the natural environment. Suggested alternatives, such as contraception and relocation, are simply not viable.

Just for the record, I produce somewhere between seven and ten tons of venison per year, and Simon's statement also explained that we don't shoot deer for commercial purposes – in other words, to sell them off for their meat. We would still have to shoot them to keep their numbers in check even if we couldn't sell them off as venison. My job and the job of the management team here is to maintain a historic herd with a bloodline that dates right back to King Henry VIII. It's animal welfare: looking after their every need. This is their home. They're born here and they die here. It's we human beings who are the aliens.

You can explain all this to people until you're blue in the face and some will still refuse to listen. Worse still, there are some folk who will go to considerable lengths to try to stop the cull. To be fair, I have not had that much trouble on a personal level from protesters – more threats than direct action – although a small group, led by a very determined individual who had been 'on our case' for years, did start waving placards around near Kingston Gate close to the house where I lived a few years ago, but there was no serious aggravation.

However, when I first started here in there had been troubles with the Animal Liberation Front, who caused all sorts of problems for us and the police. I remember that they super-glued all the locks to the park gates and daubed 'MURDERERS' in red paint on the roads. They even vandalised a local butcher's shop because he sold venison and they thought it came from the park. Their threats became serious as well, going as far as saying that they would burn down the gamekeepers' lodges. It got so bad that Scotland Yard and the CID were involved; when we went out to cull we used to take a police walkie-talkie with us and we had to keep calling in to let them know where we were in the park. Thankfully, it lasted only for that year and things quickly quietened down.

In 1985–86, Richmond had a deer 'die-off' and lost one hundred and fifty odd animals, mostly fallow bucks. I came in August 1986, just at the tail end of this period, and at the time Dave Smith, the head keeper, kept telling management that there were too many deer and not enough food, so the reason for the die-off was that they needed feeding. He kept saying to Brownie, the superintendent, 'They need feeding. They're hungry, Mr Brown.' And Brownie just kept replying, 'No, they're all right. It happens everywhere.' Management at the time were under the impression that it was a natural phenomenon and it happened in all parks, and that everything would work out OK. Well, that's true, it does – but it's at the cost of losing your older animals. It happens when they don't feed the deer until it's too late. The theory is that it's cheaper to let older animals die after the rut than to feed earlier at greater cost.

For some parks it's about economics, not the deer, but here at Richmond it's the opposite. Our primary concern is the welfare and management of an historic herd: we are not interested in economics and what we can save; it's all about the animals. Also, you have to deal with what's called 'concentration-camp syndrome', which mimics what happened at the end of World War Two, when the Allies liberated the starving prisoners from the camps and tried to feed them huge meals. This proved fatal in many cases, because their system had been devoid of food for so long that they couldn't take it. By the time you have starving deer, it's too late to feed them a normal diet because it becomes poisonous to the system. You have to get the feed into them before they are at starvation level. In Richmond, the stress of starving brought on secondary infections, which is what killed the deer in the mid-1980s.

I remember that we used to have food supplements called 'lick blocks', which were made primarily of molasses and were the shape and size of a bus wheel. It took four of us to lift them because they were so heavy. We had sixteen of them and we put them all in the back of the Land Rover. I would run the knife round the top of them because they were in plastic bags, Dave would hold the door open and I would slide one out – I couldn't lift them. Well, the deer weren't *licking* them: they were biting chunks off them! One lick block should have lasted about three months, but all sixteen went in one night. So we came back in the next morning and said, 'Look, Mr Brown, they need feeding – they've polished off all sixteen lick blocks in one night.' He still wouldn't have it.

The strange thing is that, at the time of the die-off, the park looked normal and lovely and green. But what most people don't realise is that deer are very fussy herbivores and will eat only certain grasses and herbs, and although the park looked so lush and green, the right sort of food wasn't there for them. Things got so bad that they brought in some deer experts and the summary of their findings was: you've too many deer and they are starving – exactly what Dave had been saying. At the time there were almost fifteen hundred deer in here, including more than seven hundred fallow does alone, and the herd itself shouldn't have been more than seven hundred in total. So, after all that, management decided to feed and reduce the herd, as they had recommended. Funny how management will always listen to men in suits, but never to the men 'on the floor'.

Anyway, after that, Southampton University made contact and a Professor J. Langbein (he wasn't a professor at this time: he was the student doing the study) and a Professor R. J. Putman told us they were ready to do a three-year study of our herd, and also the herd at Bushy

Park. They started it in September of that year with the male cull. It was extremely intensive: they went into everything, including grass quality, air quality, human disturbance and dog disturbance, even soil quality. They wanted samples from every animal shot during that cull and we supplied front-leg cannon bones, jawbones, three bottles of blood per animal, plus samples of liver and sometimes spleen. They also wanted the animals' bodyweight before cleaning and after, and even asked us to shoot animals of specific ages. We had to fill out reams of paperwork for each animal and much, much more.

Their report covered everything we wanted to know: how much to feed, how big a herd we could hold, when to feed and what to feed. It was so well put together that we've followed their thesis ever since and never had another die-off in the thirty years of my working at Richmond Park. I followed the thesis to the letter and we termed it our 'bible'. It really was the turning point for Richmond's deer herds. Now if we want to know anything, such as the recommended calorific intake of deer, we know where to look.

One of the things it says in the thesis is that you must start feeding the deer by 25 November, and that's one exception I have made to the rules. I extended that date by a couple of weeks, starting feeding by around 10 December, only because there's been such an explosion of acorns and beech mast in these last few years, and it's been so warm during that time that the grass has still been growing. So I felt I could get by for another couple of weeks and never had a problem. But, as I've said, the deer will let you know. That was another thing Dave told me. He said when it comes to feeding them you won't need to worry because they'll tell you. You'll go out and they'll all be chasing the Land Rover because they need food. And another time you'll get to March and put the food out and they won't even bother to get up. So that's the time to stop.

If only someone had listened to Dave in the first place, there would have been less suffering. I have said before that when I first came I would get three calls a day about deer in trouble. Towards the end, I was lucky if I got one call in three months, which is how it should be because the animals aren't here to be under pressure and suffering. When someone like the veterinary surgeon Peter Green – not only our own vet but also Advisory Veterinary Officer to the British Deer Society – says we have the finest captive red herd in the country it is praise indeed, because he covers thirty-four parks up and down the country. He tells me that some parks would still rather do things the old way and save money rather than worry about losing any animals.

THE AUTUMN CULL – HINDS AND DOES

When it comes to the cull, we start the year with a plan, which involves counting each individual animal. It sounds daunting, but it has to be done. You know you've got six hundred deer in the park by the time April comes, because the young ones haven't been born yet and you've done your two culls, so you *should* be left with the right number. But you still have to count. You have to wait until April before counting, to give last year's young males a chance to grow their antler bumps, otherwise you will not have an accurate count of males. Roughly speaking a deer herd, without natural predation, will increase by about 30 per cent per year. So to keep numbers stable you must shoot 30 per cent.

The 600 deer in Richmond Park should be an even split between fallow and red, but you might count 310 fallow and 312 red, so that's 22 animals you have to cull even before you take your 30%. There's a week's work straight away. Then you have to think, how many young will they produce? Usually, the fallow and red deer will have 100 each, in round terms. You split that in half and assume that 50 will be males and 50 females. So you'll need to lose 100 animals from each herd, plus the surplus 22. In other words you've got to shoot 110 fallow and 112 red – a total of 222 animals. That's the bare maths of the cull – not everything is as smooth as the theory dictates, however.

You get to know where certain groups of deer hang out and how they move around the park, which helps with the process. For example, you can be pretty certain that every single female fallow (doe) will be on the Flying Field because it's an open grass area and the grass grows quickest there. The reds will migrate a little, but the males will mostly stay on their stands. So, for instance, we'll start counting the bucks and there'll be a group of them near Richmond Gate, a group on the Flying Field, another on Spankers Hill, another on the camp site and one at Isabella Plantation.

Usually there'll be twenty to twenty-five in a group, but we might get to the camp site and count forty and think, there's a lot here today. And it turns out to be the Richmond Gate lot who have moved over there. That's the exception rather than the rule and, as I said, they keep to their stands more often than not. It's not that difficult, really, but then I'll get times when I'm counting and I'll see someone walking across and I'm going, 'A hundred and fifty-three, a hundred and fifty-four, a hundred and fifty-five . . .' And they'll call out, 'Hello, hello!' and I'll say, 'Can I help?' and they'll reply, 'Have you got the time, please?' So, it's back to 'One, two, three . . .'

For cull purposes the important deer are obviously red deer and fallow. These are the iconic animals that make the park what it is, and we monitor the herd every day all year round. But roe deer can be found all over the place, as can muntjac deer. I have come across the latter in Kew Gardens when I was working there. You've got all these corridors where they can roam free, for example along the Thames, Wimbledon Common and down near Esher by the M25. You can even see them in the fields near Heathrow Airport at five in the morning. Muntjac are all around us and they often give birth to twins. In one year a female can have twins and before the year is out those two youngsters could themselves be pregnant with twins. They're the one deer species that doesn't have a season because they can breed all year round. That means that, unlike fallow and red, you can shoot them all year round.

The annual cull of deer happens in two stages: first in November, when we cull the females, and then in February, when we cull the male population. When I first came to the park, August was the month that we started the cull, since the open season for male deer is from 1 August to 30 April. Things have moved on since then and now we cull the males in February, which isn't the ideal time to do it, but it's all we have open to us.

The season for females is much shorter - only from 1 November to 31 March. It's as important to shoot does and hinds as stags and bucks. Female numbers determine the size of the herd. But the cull is never simple: you need to shoot them early or you'll be killing animals with well-developed young inside them. The fewer females you have, the smaller your cull will be. However, nowadays at Richmond, we get six weeks at best in which to get the cull done, as it is a public park and we can't stay shut for ever.

We used to begin at 3 a.m., which is a godawful time to start because you're managing only a few hours' sleep a night and constantly feeling tired. They still cull like this at Bushy Park and it means that you don't need a night licence to do your cull because it's considered daytime culling in law. Here at Richmond, because of public safety and the fact that we have a much bigger park and herd, we can cull only at night, so a licence is needed.

But because we culled so late at night, it made a difference to the shooting problems, notably when autumn arrived and things changed. For example, there was often a mist or fog at night and it was really perturbing as you saw it begin to cover the park. Some nights there was a thick mist about four feet high from the floor, which meant you could see the animal's head for shooting purposes but not its body. The first night the mist rose that high, we shot a couple of deer, which promptly fell and were hidden by the mist. When you're working at night you get a little disoriented: things aren't always where you think they are and distances change. So we spent the next hour trying to find those two, because now they were totally hidden by the mist.

Then, on another night, you could see their bodies but not their heads, so you couldn't shoot them at all. We had other nights when there were layers of mist only a foot deep hovering off the floor, but moving up and down and intertwining with other layers. Without seeing it with the naked eye it's difficult to describe, but it really was spooky to be out there at night. Another time, the fog was so thick that we had to abandon the cull for that night because, when a spotlight hits fog, all you can see in your scope is a big white blanket. I can remember being on the Flying Field and having a real task trying to get off and back onto the road because of really thick fog.

They would be really long nights then because you

started at midnight and wouldn't finish until about 9 a.m. We had to skin every animal, and even a small fallow doe would take thirty to forty minutes to clean from start to finish. When there were ten other animals lying on the floor outside, you knew that there were another five to six hours of skinning and cleaning to do, so a long night was inevitable. Nowadays, the animals are sold in their skin, but we still have to clean them, which is one hell of a job and definitely not for the squeamish.

When the dead animal is brought in we pull it up on a winch and bleed it by opening up the main artery on the neck, because the cavity in the chest is full of blood. Next we take the animal's back legs off up to the knee and then we might take the front legs off to the knee as well. Then we run a knife down the belly line and its stomach, intestines and spleen all come out, which leaves a wall of flesh making up the diaphragm. The other side of that you've got the lungs and the heart, which all have to be removed, as do the anus, bladder, testicles and so forth.

You spread the stomach and intestines out, which are like webbing, and you're looking at the lymph nodes and glands to search for any signs of disease, especially notifiable diseases such as TB and bluetongue. There are so many new diseases coming along that are all heading our way. You'd know if one of the deer was bad because the lymph nodes, especially up on the groin, would be swollen. I've had deer with broken legs and the lymph nodes were huge because they were fighting infection.

The next job is to saw through the sternum, run a

knife down the spine and remove everything that's left, including the heart, head, lungs and trachea. Then the carcass has a leg tag put on it with a barcode that might bear my or Tony's ID, depending on who's been shooting that night. It's all about traceability. You're signing off the carcass. You have to say what it is: for example a red stag, the date it was shot, the time it was shot; you're also saying that it's fit for consumption. It then gets sent off and the vet at the abattoir or the processing plant inspects it and, if he finds something wrong, it can be traced back to us.

There's buckets of blood and you're covered in it from head to toe. If you don't like the sight or the smell of blood, it's best to get out or you'll be on the deck. And, believe me, I've had men floating around on the floor in all sorts of messes. I've had big burly coppers down here who have said, 'Oh, yes, I'm fine with all that blood-and-guts stuff.' And the next thing you know they've keeled over and are lying flat on their face. It's not just the blood and gore: it's all the smells you get when an animal is opened up.

I suppose I'm lucky because none of that stuff has ever bothered me, even when I first started, including the smells you get from fish, which are far worse than anything else. I was once called out to deal with a dead carp that was floating on Pen Ponds. It had been lying in the sun for ages and it had blown up like a beach ball. I went to get it with my net and a stick and it just went *pop*: all the goo poured out and the smell was unbelievable.

If anybody comes here now, male or female, I say the same thing to them: 'If you're going to feel queasy, for goodness' sake say something. Don't try to brave it out because if you fall over you could hit something and end up in serious trouble, not to mention getting covered in blood. And, if you're going to be sick, please go and be sick outside, because if you vomit in here I'll have to condemn the animal, burn it and throw it away, which is a waste.' It's the same with Tony and me: if we've got gastric problems or flu we can't cull; we're not allowed to come in because it's transferable.

You can be as careful as you like and still end up in trouble. As I write this, we've just had a new floor put down in the venison house ready for the cull in November. This came about because I nearly ended up in hospital after slipping on the floor and bringing down a stainless steel table on top of me, just missing my head. The floor had been painted the month before with special non-slip coating and was supposed to be the dog's doodahs, but it didn't work because when it got wet it was more like an ice rink. And the floor is always wet in the venison house, with either blood or water, so management had to have a rethink and hopefully the new floor is the real deal. So now Tony and I have got to put back everything that we need for the cull – tables, freezers and so forth – but bearing in mind that I won't be here as I'll be retired by then, it should be finished off by Tony and the new person who takes over Tony's old position.

Another strict rule we have is that if one of us is

behaving out of character, it has to be reported. So, for example, if Tony came in one day and started doing silly things I'd have to notify management and tell them that he seemed to be under pressure. And he'd have to do the same if it was I who started acting funny. You can't be too careful in our line of work because we carry deadly weapons. It's up to management to decide what they're going to do and it's not about informing: it's about being responsible and watching out for one another. You never know what people are going through in their personal lives. They could be under huge strain and the last thing you want is a man who carries knives and guns to be stressed out.

Just about everything we do is covered by some kind of rule or regulation, which is for everyone's benefit. The law covering deer and pheasants and other wildlife is always changing and is as fluid as the ripples on Pen Ponds. For example, one recent law is that everyone who deals with rat and mouse poison has to have a relevant certificate. We do use rat poison here, so people such as Tony will have to do whatever's necessary to achieve that certificate in order to carry on doing that aspect of the job.

When I look back, I can hardly believe what I was called on to do just two days after taking on the job in 1986 (in those days the cull was done in August). I'd shot deer before but never on that scale. However, because the herd in Richmond Park had been allowed to build up – with seven hundred does instead of around two hundred – I had to shoot five hundred animals. Those were the days when you were expected to begin the cull at 3 a.m., and you worked seven days a week. Now, at least, I have weekends off to recover.

When I first got the job I was full of excitement because I didn't know what to expect; it was all new to me. After a week of twenty-four seven culling, I soon realised that it had become an endurance test and I didn't really have a lot of time to reflect on shooting deer. Throughout the years there have been several occasions when I have felt sadness and have shed tears for an animal that has been put to death – I wouldn't be human if I didn't – like when I have seen babies standing over a dead mother's body after she's been run over. At times, I have seen injuries to animals that were so shocking I have had to look away.

Many times, I have been with Dave Smith, Kia Handley or Tony Hatton during the cull when we've had numerous animals in front of us and haven't been able to decide which one to shoot. We'll choose one and then say 'No, it's too nice an animal to kill'. And then the same thing has happened two or three times and we've found that the deer have all walked off because we couldn't make up our minds. There's always a tinge of sadness when you have to take out such lovely animals, but in terms of necessity, there is a lot of truth in what Spock is always saying in *Star Trek*: 'The needs of the many outweigh the needs of the few'. To keep a herd the size of the one at Richmond in optimum condition, there will always be some deer that need to go.

There's a lot to the cull. You don't just go out and shoot the first animal you see with a bit of a limp. You've got to work out a spectrum of ages. You don't want to take out a whole generation: you want a range of animals from six months right through to twelve-, thirteen- and fourteen-year-olds. It's very selective: you're trying to take out the worst one each time. It's like trying to emulate what a pack of wolves would do in the wild. On average, 60 per cent of the cull will be between one and four; and 40 per cent will be between five and maturity, which will include animals from ten upwards.

With the females, it's very difficult to age them. I can pick a yearling out, but anything past two is difficult. I had a hind here once that looked only about four years old, but I knew she was twenty-seven and a half because she had an ear tag from birth. She missed the record for the oldest deer in the country by about six months. Without a tag to go by, it's down to experience – you have to go by body mass. Think of a young woman, eighteen to twenty years old, beautiful in face and figure. By middle age she's starting to get a bit plump, her hair's going grey, she's walking with a stoop. Now project ahead to when she's eighty: she's on a Zimmer frame; she can just about walk. It's the same with deer. You get a young female with a lovely slender neck. She looks like a ballerina. As she becomes middle-aged she gets a bit plump and it shows in her face. And, as she gets even older, she sags and struggles to get about.

Because you can never be totally accurate about their

age, I divide them into those that look young, middle-aged and old, and, out of my cull of, say, a hundred animals, I would select thirty young ones, twenty-five or thirty middle-aged and forty old ones, so you've got a spectrum. But with the males, because they've got antlers, you can tell which ones are yearlings and which are old, and you can age them from one to ten. So, before we cull the males, we'll go out and count how many yearlings we've got, how many twos, threes, fours and so on.

We use a system known as the Hoffman Pyramid, which means you have the oldest animal at the top of the triangle and the youngest at the bottom. If you have a bulge in the middle you know you've got to cull more six and seven-year-olds to redress the balance. You're looking to take out the worst one each time, so, for example, if I see a female with a floppy ear, she's marked out straight away. Basically, I'm looking for a reason to take them out because the animals have been so well managed that almost every single one is A1 quality. But you have to take them; you don't have a choice. You've got to get their numbers down. It's easier with the stags because you can look at their antlers. So you might think, look at him, he's smashed all his antlers on one side; he's got to go.

Sometimes I'll have three brockets, which are little yearlings with spikes, standing alongside one another, but one of them will be really small-bodied, which means he's a late calf, and late calves never make good animals. So you look out for things like that. And also you might have an animal with a cataract, or an abscess, or a severe limp, or a deep wound where he's cut himself on something. There are always odds and sods that you can pick, although they're few and far between.

In general, females are more difficult to cull, especially fallow does. They're very flighty. If you shoot one, the rest will all run off; it's very rare that you'll get two on the same spot. This means that I'll often be down on my numbers and I'll have to take heart shots from a distance, which I don't like doing because it means that you've got to cut off the front half of the animal and throw it away because it's been destroyed. The reds are not such a problem – males and females – because they tend to stay together even when you start shooting them. I've gone out and shot six red hinds all standing on the same spot in five minutes.

Before the start of the cull I'll have worked out that I need to shoot, say, 110 females for that cull. Then I'll calculate how many nights I need in November, and, if I get through into the first week of December, I'll work out how many animals that means per night. Let's say it's five a night – that means that, in theory, I mustn't drop below five. But then I might get out there and find there's thick fog; I can't see in front of my face, so I'll have to abandon it. Sometimes I can get all the animals shot in fifteen minutes, but other nights I'll just have a devil of a job reaching the number. I've been out there on occasions for three hours and I've got only two, which means I'm three behind schedule. If I add in the night I didn't shoot any because of the fog, I'm eight behind, which means I'm now playing serious catch-up.

In terms of overall numbers, we run a ratio of two females to one male, and we allow for about three acres to each animal. That's a good amount of space and that's the way it should be, because they're herding animals and they like to roam about, so you don't want them all cramped up.

You can have a ratio of one male to one female, but there is scientific evidence to show that if you do that the males would spend more time fighting than bonking, so the number of births would not be as good. They've found that, if you have a ratio of two to one you have a much better birth rate. You can, theoretically, have ten females to one male, and we had it at three to one for a while because we had to supply the Royal Warrant, which was stopped by Tony Blair's government when Labour came to power in 1997. (Mind you, it's been stopped five times in its history and it's been started five times in its history. So, when a new government comes into power, one of the ministers might look at the books and say, 'Do you realise we can get a free leg of venison?' and the law could be changed again.)

When we had three females to one male, we were having massive culls – around two hundred and eighty a year. So one day I said to Simon Richards, the superintendent, 'Look, this is stupid. Why don't we drop back to two to one? That means you'll have a hundred fewer females and therefore have sixty fewer young, and you'll have a smaller cull of around a hundred and eighty to two hundred.' It's made quite a difference.

The more females you have, the more young you have, and therefore the bigger the cull. The females control the herd number. For example, if you do your cull this year and you haven't managed to shoot twenty females, you might think, that's OK – I'll leave them till next year. But they're all pregnant, so you haven't left twenty: you've left forty, because they're all going to produce young. So next year, instead of one week's work, you've got two weeks' work before you even start on next year's cull figure. Talk about compound interest.

PLANNING AHEAD – NEW BEASTS, NEW GENES

We are always looking to the future of the herd. In order to keep the deer herd fit and healthy, with no threat of weakness or deformity through inbreeding, Richmond Park has always moved livestock to and from the park. I have records of fallow deer being moved from park to park as far back as 1650. This is essential to keep the bloodline moving, so every twenty-five to thirty years we get in a couple of new males.

Previously, we'd always gone to Windsor Great Park and Bushy Park, but back in 2004, the last time we added new stags, we felt it was time to go further afield, so I found a place in Norfolk run by a guy called Jamie Ellis at Gunton Park. When I went up there and saw the size of their stags and bucks I was blown away. They looked fantastic: their stature, antlers and body size were really impressive. We purchased one red stag and one fallow buck. Both were about three to four years old, breeding animals ready to do their jobs.

When we brought them back to Richmond Park they were put into Pen Ponds Plantation for safety and to acclimatise – which proved to be a total waste of time. When I went to check on them the next morning, they'd both escaped and were running all over the place, bossing the rest of the herd around as if they had been there for years.

You only need the two males to bonk a dozen females each in the first rut and the job is done, as the new-born deer will have new blood. This actually happened with their first rut that year. And they continued bossing the other males around for the next eight years, producing countless numbers of progeny. They must have thought they had died and gone to heaven.

The next time new blood needs bringing in will be around 2030, by which time I'll be long gone. But an awful lot will happen before I wave the old place goodbye and Tony steps into my well-worn shoes.

WINTER FEEDING

As winter begins to take a grip and the park is covered in a silvery cloak of frost, the trees look spindly and lifeless and the grass stops growing, which means the deer lose a vital natural food source. But not everything is bleak as they huddle together for warmth. The perennial cycle of nature is beginning to make its presence felt in the female deer with signs of new birth beginning to show. The females are approaching halfway through their pregnancies; some are already looking bloated, although most won't really start showing until around April or May.

All that Mother Earth can throw at the deer in terms of weather has little effect on the animals themselves. Deer are extremely robust animals and, in general, our winters have little effect because most years they are relatively mild.

In terms of the food that is available, some years there is an abundance of acorns, which come in such vast numbers that the deer gorge themselves. I have seen does die of tannin poisoning. This is where the animal eats a lot over a short space of time. Acorns from British oaks can be particularly toxic to them. If the acorns came sporadically and the deer ate them gradually they would be okay – it's simply too many in one go that kills them.

Other than that, food is short in winter but the animals are fed every night to replace the lack of vitamins and proteins. Spring is what I call the 'juicy green time': all the trees and shrubs take on a very vibrant green and look good to eat. The foliage is all fresh and new before it becomes browned by the heat of summer. It's also the time for flowers like primroses and cherry blossom.

In contrast, summer is hard for the animals. You have to realise that we can take our coats off, but deer can't.

They spend a lot of their time sitting under trees trying to keep cool. The grass becomes living hay and turns white as the sun bleaches it. The stags have put on so much weight that they have to be careful that they don't overheat. Autumn is wonderful for everything – for colour and for stags fighting and roaring – but it's also a time of plenty for the deer with lots of appetizing foodstuffs like blackberries, horse chestnuts, acorns and beech mast.

Most of January is spent cleaning the venison house in preparation for the second stage of the cull, checking traps dotted around the park, and monitoring the herd every day to see if they are alright. It's a funny time of year: it doesn't get light until eight in the morning and it's already getting dark by 4 p.m., so not a lot can be done in the short daylight hours.

At this time of year you have to remember that the rut finished back in October and they're on their winter feed. When the grass stops growing it's very meagre out there for all wild animals, not just deer. All the insects have gone, all the seeds have gone, so animals are really having to scrimp and scrape just to get enough calories to keep going. That's why it's always wise to keep a close eye on them. The deer migrate more in the winter months – that is to say they move all around the park looking for pastures new. And they're very fussy herbivores. They're like mice; they nibble at a bit of everything: grass, seeds, hay, a few leaves, a bit of bramble, a few flowers. They won't just stand there and chomp away nonstop at grass like sheep.

In winter we work a split shift because we have to come back in the late evening to feed the herd, which is done seven days a week from the end of November through to the end of March. There's always office work to be done and various meetings to attend. We have what is called an estates meeting every month, which is basically a team meeting where everyone comes in to discuss issues that are coming up in the near future that we might be involved in, as well as works such as the maintenance of offices, buildings or houses in the park. And there's recently been a lot of talk about what will happen when we become a charitable trust.

As we get near to Christmas, we have to try to work out our rota, as we take it in turns each year to do Christmas and New Year on call. Every other year we get that period off, which makes it fair for all wildlife officers. We still have to do the deer feed every night, but on some occasions, members of management take over that job so that we are off completely.

In January 2016 we had only one callout, which was for a dead fallow deer, who had been stabbed in the side by a buck or a young pricket – a second-year male fallow deer. What probably happened was that she came into season late, which can happen occasionally, and two bucks or prickets were fighting over her, trying to mate. Prickets have spikes on the fronts of their heads and they can be lethal if they pierce another animal in the wrong place.

We usually find about half a dozen deer that have died fighting during the course of the winter. I remember once

71

PARK LIFE

I came across two bucks that had been fighting and ended up with a piece of rope that was dangling from a tree tied to their antlers (don't ask me how that happened!). Every time the pair of them started running they would swing around the tree until the rope tightened up and then they would run back the other way. It was as if they were on a maypole. Trying to shoot a deer when it's going round in endless circles is almost impossible. I managed to do it, but it was nerve-racking, I can tell you.

THE SPRING CULL – STAGS AND BUCKS

We begin the second round of the cull – for the male deer – at the end of January, which means Tony and I have to adapt to another six weeks of working nights (as with hinds, the cull is carried out at night for health and safety reasons). It's not easy, especially as other staff think you're still working nine to five and ring you up just when you're trying to catch up on sleep! As well as Richmond Park, we have to cull the deer at Greenwich Park. February is not the ideal time to cull males. Really, they should be culled in August to take out all the animals that won't be good enough to breed with in October. Also, the animals are at their heaviest in August, which would mean more money from selling them off as venison. Each animal will have lost anything up to fifty kilos in weight over the winter; plus, it is still light at 5 a.m. in August, which would mean the animals wouldn't get alarmed by the bright spotlight that we do have to use when we cull through the night.

A fortnight before culling, we 'zero' the rifles, the .243 and the .308, which means accurately aligning the sights and the scope so that the bullets go where the crosshairs are. We have a site in the park at Oak Lodge dump, where we have big mounds, which are actually giant manure heaps, and we put a target up and try to get the shots in a circle that's no bigger than about three inches across (two inches if possible) from a distance of eighty yards.

They always say that, whatever you spend on a gun, you spend twice that amount on the scope. The one I use cost £3,500 six years ago and only £1,000 of that was for the gun itself. In this country the law states that you can't go any smaller than a .240, and it must have a muzzle energy of 1,700 foot-pounds.

This requirement comes from the Deer Society, because back in the sixties, if you were out shooting pigeons or rabbits anywhere in the country with a scatter gun and a deer ran across your path you could have a swing at it. Many people did and on many occasions a deer would run away and die very slowly with buckshot up its backside. So the Deer Society put pressure on the government to stop people using guns firing tiny bullets, which would just wound the animals. When the law was brought in they also included rules about seasons, because people had been shooting at the wrong time of year. For example, they'd shoot a female in June when she'd just dropped a calf and she was in full milk; nobody knew where it was, so it would die as well.

My bullets are .243 calibre and doing something like 2,700 feet per second (fps) in the first 100 yards. Tony's are doing something like 3,500 feet per second. The theory is that the shot is so instantaneous that the deer can't move before it's hit, but sometimes they do move at the last moment.

A head shot, which is the equivalent of that small circle of about three inches across, is the worst type of shot because you have to be so precise. You've got to hit the deer between the eye and the ear; that's all you've got to aim at. I never aim between the eyes because a deer has a long nose and, if it lifts its head up just when you pull the trigger, your four-inch target becomes a half-inch bar and the bullet will travel up its nose – which won't be a fatal shot.

If the animal is looking away from me I'll put my horizontal line across its ears. It has a black dorsal stripe running down the middle of its back, so it's like a cross, which I've put right between the ears. That's the best shot of the lot. We use what are known as 'expanding-head bullets', which have a copper jacket and a special soft lead core. This means that when the bullet goes in, it breaks into thousands of tiny pieces and they're all travelling at 2,000 fps inside the head, so death is instantaneous; there's no chance the deer is going to get up. You're only allowed to use a solid bullet in war because the aim is simply to take the enemy out of the battle, not to do disfiguring, devastating damage; a solid bullet will go in and come out the other side, leaving two small holes, if it doesn't hit a bone. Our expanding-head bullets make a small hole initially but then widen out and leave a huge cavity, so, if you shoot a deer from behind, the top of the head will be completely missing.

When you're training for deer management your trainers advocate that you go for a heart shot because you've got a ten-inch killing circle. So if you miss the heart you'll hit the lungs; if you miss the lungs you'll hit the liver or the spleen. You'll hit one of the vital organs, or more than one, and it won't go far; it will drop. But if I could take a head shot from behind, I would take it every time because it's instantaneous and the name of the game is to cause as little suffering as possible. A side head shot isn't so good because the animal can lift its head at the vital moment.

Before I go out culling every night at Richmond and Greenwich I have to inform the police. They have to know because otherwise they might get people ringing in saying, 'There's some bloke out there with a gun.' They'll hear bangs in the background and the next thing you know coppers will be dropping out of helicopters. That has happened. I've had them dropping out of a helicopter with all their gear on saying, 'Have you got two blokes in a Land Rover shooting deer?' We've said, 'We phoned through and told you about it.' And they've replied, 'Well, we didn't get the message.' I have to ring them every night when I go out during the six weeks I'm culling and then I have to ring them back and tell them when I've finished.

I also have to notify them when I'm going out with a gun for any other purpose, such as pest control.

For example, if I'm going to Greenwich to do the cull there, I phone in and they give me a CAD (computer-aided dispatch) number and then they inform all the Met police within that area. If someone rings in and says, 'I'm next to Greenwich Park and I can hear gunshots,' they know it's me through the CAD number. When I ring them back to tell them that I've put the guns away, they can close that CAD down. I usually joke with them by saying, 'If you hear any gunshots now, it's not me, so get the army out.'

Culling deer with a high-powered rifle has problems in itself, quite apart from the actual business of trying to kill as instantly and humanely as possible. Ammunition today is accurate and dangerous to a mile, but will probably go three miles, so you have to think all the time about where the bullet's going to end up if you miss, because it won't stop until it hits something. Expanding-head bullets are designed to stay in the body and not come out the other side, but you can't rely on that, so safety is a real issue when we are shooting deer at Richmond and Greenwich. We have all of suburbia around us and it is obviously vital that bullets stay in the park.

I knew a man who started his professional life as a dog boy on a country estate. He then served his time, went to war, became a Royal Marine and fought in big campaigns in World War Two. A Royal Marine has to be able to break down any weapon – of enemy or ally – clean it, put it back together and operate it. This man had forgotten more about guns than I'll ever know about them. He became a head keeper for the Royal Parks and did a deer cull in Bushy Park. He took what he thought was a safe shot with a tree crate behind the animal, but the bullet went right through the deer, hit the crate, bounced and went out of the park and in through someone's window.

A bullet that is tumbling or ricocheting can do far more damage than one that flies straight, because it's coming in at a different angle, and he was incredibly lucky that no one was hurt. That happened twice to him in a fortnight and he said to me, 'You try convincing people you're a safe shot after that's happened twice.' That's why I say to everyone here, 'Never get cocky with a gun. You might think you've taken a safe shot but you never know for certain.' Our guns are accurate to a mile and they will kill to a mile, so you can never be too careful. That's why we stand up and shoot from a turret in the Land Rover because, by doing so, we're directing our shot downwards.

This poses a particular problem when we cull at Greenwich, because the deer paddock is on top of a hill, so I have to make sure I line up the deer I'm going to shoot against the backdrop of a tree or something solid. If I didn't do that, and missed the deer, I could end up bumping off someone in an office twenty floors up in Canary Wharf Tower, which is just across the Thames and well within range of my bullet. Furthermore, although they're in a paddock, they've gone feral and they run in a pack, and the one I'm looking for will often be smack in the middle. There have been times when I've just lined one up to shoot and a double-decker bus has turned up on the road that runs on the other side of the wall. I've been able to see the people on the top deck all staring, with their jaws dropping, saying, 'Look at that guy with a gun!' So I've dropped down out of sight waiting for a siren to go off and the police to come whizzing round the corner. All in all, it's a nightmare.

In the old days, one of the keepers would climb a tree to shoot, so, if he missed, his bullet would end up in the ground. But in order to do that, he had to start and finish shooting in daylight. Can you imagine me doing that nowadays? I'd be on the front pages of the *Sun* and the *Daily Mirror* and on the television news, and the police would probably be out hunting for me after people phoned in to say there's a madman on the loose with a gun in the Park.

When we start culling in the last week of January the carcasses hang in the larder until the first Friday in February, which is when the dealer comes (he comes every Friday for six weeks). I can store them for ten days because I've got enough room to store thirty-six carcasses. The dealer signs them off to say they're OK and any contamination from that point is down to him; but, because of the leg-tagging system, which carries a barcode, any problems can be traced back to me. So if one turns out to have tuberculosis and the meat ends up poisoning a dozen people in a restaurant, I'm the one who'll end up in court because I've certified that it's fit for consumption. I don't want to sound complacent, but in all the years I've been here nothing like that has ever happened.

I can usually tell you if an animal needs to be condemned the moment I run a knife down its belly. Just from the look of it I'll say, 'This one needs to go in the burner,' and then we'll have to wash the whole room down and spray it with disinfectant. It's just something I've developed an instinct for because I've done so many over the years. That said, the problem with animals is that they're covered in fur, so they can look absolutely fine. I've opened one up that looked in perfect condition, and it'd had all its ribs busted on one side where a car must have hit it and there was a two-litre bag of brown fluid floating in there where the lungs should have been.

In terms of the commercial process involved in the sell-off of the venison, it begins with the office manager putting out tenders, and then wholesalers from all over the country send in letters saying how much they're going to give us per kilo. The letters are kept in a safe and all opened at the same time, with two witnesses to make sure everything is above board, and whoever has put in the best price gets the contract.

You'll still find the odd stag in January who'll be roaring and chasing the girls, but they're middle-aged stags having a bit of a crisis. The masters have all had enough by now. They're worn out and they've got injuries to recover from, but even more, they need to recover from the sleep deprivation, which is vast. During the rut they simply can't afford to sleep because, if they do fall asleep, they'll lose their harem; and, if they lose their harem, they've got no one to breed with. So it's all about staying awake and keeping off every other stag that comes within their patch. When you see them lying around like fat hippos in the summer there's a reason for that, because when the rut's over every ounce of that fat has gone and somehow they have to get through winter.

We usually start the cull in Richmond on the first Monday in February. Don't ask me why; it's just a tradition. That involves working right through the night. Our body clocks are all over the place but we still have to come back in during the day to select animals for culling, check traps and do office work. We have six weeks at best to finish the culling and it's pretty full on because we need to make sure we don't drop below the figures we've worked out for each night.

We shoot the deer *in situ* in the park rather than rounding them up. This could take a couple of hours because we have to find the ones we've marked down for culling. Once they've been shot, they're bled, dragged into the trailer and brought back to the venison house for cleaning. They are then pushed through into the chiller until the dealer comes. Our vet, Peter Green, comes out on the cull to assess our culling methods and the condition of the animals. He takes away samples from all carcasses to test for any problems. In all the years he's been coming, we've never had a bad report.

Peter, who is the advisory vet for the British Deer Association, took over from a man called Michael Simons, who had done the job for nearly sixty years and was in his nineties. I said to Simon Richards, the superintendent, 'We've got to get a new vet because we never see Michael Simons down here.' Simon asked me if I had any ideas about whom we might get and I replied, 'Well, it's got to be somebody who knows about deer. It's no good going to the local vet. He's all right with Rover the dog, Tiddles the cat and Bert the budgie, but, when it comes to something specialised like this, he won't have a clue.'

When I phoned Peter up and told him who I was and asked him if he'd be prepared to pick up the baton and be our vet, Peter said, 'I'll give you a provisional yes but I want to come down and see your herd and I want to watch you cull.' I could understand that because he had a reputation to maintain. However, he was so impressed with what he saw that he brought a colleague back to watch us carrying out the cull and said, 'I've never seen anything like it in my life. This place is unique.' Last year, he told Simon, 'You've got the finest herd of captive red deer I've ever seen.'

There could be no finer compliment than that.

AFTER THE CULL – MARCH AND APRIL

The stags begin casting their antlers in February, the oldest ones being the first to lose them. They have four feet of new antler to grow in six months. It's like a child's new tooth: the old one is falling out and a new one is coming through. In the early stages, you can bend the antler: it's covered in a membrane like velvet and full of blood vessels. It can easily snap and fall down like a blood bag and if it sets it will become permanently deformed.

When the stags have cast their antlers they mix with the females for the simple reason that they look a bit like females. That means payback time for the young stags: you've beaten the hell out of me all summer – now it's my turn. As I've said before, deer don't deliberately set out to kill their rivals: what they're really trying to do is intimidate them enough to make them move away from the area. Stags know that as soon as a rival has cast he's defenceless, and it's inevitable that on occasions the older one will end up being seriously hurt or killed by a young pretender. I've seen the chaos when a master buck's lost his antlers – he's trying to get away and they're chasing him at full pelt – they're determined they're going to get him. They're trying to give him hell – stab him up the backside and everything else.

At this time of year the young ones have the advantage because they cast last. The older ones have much more antler to grow, so that's why they cast first. The old antler comes away completely. They've got two stumps called pedicles on their heads and the antler falls off at the pedicle. Within twenty-four hours you'll see a slight bump raised: the new growth has started already. And within the first week, they'll have two bumps about two inches long. The antlers continue to grow, about two to two and half inches a week, but accidents do happen and you'll see some stags with antlers that have snapped and become permanently deformed; these have to be culled.

I've got one young brocket now that's snapped one side off and looks like a unicorn. You daren't leave them because, at least when they've got two antlers and they go to fight another stag, they can lock. With just one, they can go straight through the middle and do serious damage. Tony will have to take him out when I'm gone and when he's culling the females in November, in order to get him out of the way and prevent him injuring too many other males.

Every year, as they get older, the antlers get bigger and better and more majestic, but they'll hit a peak age when, instead of getting bigger, the growth will go the other way. So you'll have one side that's perfect and looks fantastic and the other side will be all deformed. I've always called it 'going back' and it's based on the hormone testosterone, which is why you can't castrate them. People sometimes say, 'Why don't you just castrate them and then they won't rut and you won't have to worry about them having young?' I tell them that as soon as a castrated stag has cast his antlers, he'll never grow another pair and he won't roar or fight or any of the other natural things. If a male deer gets whacked in his testicles when he's very young the antlers can become deformed.

There are some parks that breed their stags specifically for what's known as a gold-medal head (part of a national awards scheme). Some of them have got so many spikes that they look totally abnormal. I would rather a stag had a lovely wide beam with six tines on each side than sixty-six. If you could see some of them you'd say, 'What on earth's happened there?' They look bizarre.

The process of antler-casting is one of several changes I've noticed in the deer since I've been here. Now they start casting in the first week of February, whereas it used to be well into March. It's the same with what's known as 'clean antler' – when the antler is fully developed – which used to happen in August and now happens in July. Whether it's climate change or something else I don't know, but things are definitely changing.

In 2016, they started casting their antlers in January before we'd even started culling. I've never known that happen before. And because of that I said to Tony, 'You know what's going to happen? They're going to start fraying really early, around the beginning of July probably.' Fraying is when the blood vessels shrink, the blood flow stops and the velvet cracks and frays; it's like shards of flesh hanging over their antlers. Anyway, talk about making me look a liar. They didn't start fraying until the first week of August.

They're definitely casting earlier, though. When we used to cull in August, all the antlers, during the first ten days at least, would have to be buried because they were still covered in velvet and we're not allowed to sell them in velvet. The clean antler wouldn't start coming in until the second week. Now they're all in clean antler before August.

When I first came here we used to sell the whole lot: antlers, cannon bones, tendons on the backs of the legs, which are used to make the strings on violin bows, offal, genitals, stags' tusks (rounded teeth that look like pearls) in pairs, tails, skin – everything. Nowadays you can't *give* most of it away, although antlers still sell well and can make anything from £70 to £250. You've got to remember that there's a lot of work involved in the preparation: the head's got to be cut off, then it's got to be skinned, boiled and washed, and everything has to be removed to leave just the antlers and the skull plate. It's two days' work for one person.

As March rolls around, the cull finally ends and Tony and I spend the next couple of weeks readjusting our bodies to normal sleeping and eating patterns. We have numerous jobs to carry out in the venison house, including boiling stags' heads so they're ready for sale. This involves boning out the head, boiling off what flesh is left and cutting down through the skull so what's left is a plate, which has the antlers on top of it. Then we bleach the finished article to make it perfectly white. After that it's cleaning and tidying up before we shut down completely until the next cull.

During the last few days of March we return to our normal duties: pest control; checking traps; filing all relevant records of the cull on the computer, which can take a week; team meetings to catch up on what's been happening; and finishing the deer feeding. In 2016, when Peter Green sent in his veterinary report, it read very well, as it always has done so far. He noted that fat levels were very good again, so we had nothing to worry about for another year.

The deer sometimes get a touch of fur lice at this time of year and can look as if they're going bald, but all the bald patches disappear when the new summer coat comes through. In general, it's a quiet time of year. All the males bar a few have cast their antlers and it's all about getting fat and lazy for the summer – all for a good reason, as we have already seen. Meanwhile, the females are getting on for six months pregnant and looking bloated.

We finish the daily feeding for the deer in April, having begun it in November. The deer will let you know when they want it and also when they've had enough. For example, in 2015 we were culling deer in November and were out on the Flying Field when we saw some we wanted to shoot and turned the spotlight on them. Suddenly, deer began running towards us from all directions, males and females. They thought we were going to start feeding, because we put the lights on when we feed. Normally we call them and they come running. I said to Tony, 'Just bear this in mind. They let you know when they want it and they'll let you know when they don't.'

There have been times at the end of March when I've called them and put the back lights on and they just stay sitting there. So I've put the corn and the pellets out but they still don't move. I've come back the next morning and the food is still lying there totally untouched; they didn't want it. When this happens you know you don't need to do it anymore because there's enough natural food for them in the park. It depends to a large extent on the weather: if there's enough warmth in the ground and the grass has started to grow, and if there are enough buds around, then they've got what they need.

The most important thing is getting them over the hurdle of the winter period, especially the males, because, as we have seen, they use up all their fat reserves during the rut and they have nothing left. But they're very tough, resilient animals. They can live with injuries that you wouldn't believe. If they were human males they'd be in hospital, dying or dead. In contrast, the females are blooming because they're pregnant and they've got plenty of fat on them.

CALVING – MAY

As May rolls around, we are into what I call 'Ooo-aaah' time, when the first young animals emerge into the world. Most of the calves and fawns are born in June. Calves are red deer babies and fawns are fallow. Red deer rut first, so their young are born earlier than the fallow, usually by about three weeks. This is the only time deer ever eat meat, when the new mothers eat the placenta. It's a built-in safety device, originally to protect against wolves in the wild by leaving no evidence of birth. As soon as the calves are born they're licked off and dried off. They can stand up right away and they can run from birth as well. But they usually spend most of the first week sleeping.

The mothers will come back from grazing every couple of hours or so to feed the new-borns. They have to make sure to feed themselves properly as they need to produce as much quality milk as possible. Although it might be tempting for deer lovers to sneak a close-up, it's best to stay well clear. If the young deer bleats you're in trouble, especially if you've got a dog. A protective mother will happily chase a careless dog-walker all the way through the park.

I used to have to keep a diary detailing everything I'd done during each month, and it was all recorded by Brownie, the superintendent, and put on file – although I never found out exactly what he did with all the info. One year I wrote 'May' and added 'hem' on the end because it really was mayhem. On the 25th, the new generation all decided that was the day they were going to be born. I had new-borns popping out all over the place: some were half in and half out; some were dead; some were stillborn. We used to dart the mother in those cases and we would pull her young out while she was unconscious and leave it with her to give her a chance to realise it was dead before we took it away.

Brownie, or Michael Baxter Brown, to give him his full name, served twenty years in the park and was a bit of a character. Hearsay had it that he had managed a tea plantation in India before he took on the Richmond job. Brownie was a formidable boss but he was actually a very nice guy, and I had a lot of time for him because he gave me my big chance in life. He wrote a book called *Richmond Park: The History of a Royal Deer Park* and also used to write articles for the British Deer Society's journal.

Watching the new-born calves is something that I still find magical after all these years. You'd have to have a very hard heart not to feel moved when you see those gorgeous little creatures emerge into the world trying to find their feet, wobbling and tottering about, looking like they're all legs and ears. They don't eat solid food at all while they're suckling and they're usually weaned off by November.

In most cases, births are straightforward, but you can get complications. The young are born feet first and their heads are pointing towards their feet, but not so long ago I came across a baby that had turned its head sideways in the birth canal and its nose had hit the wall of the canal, so it was stuck and had suffocated. All you could see was one ear, and its feet were hanging out, so its mother couldn't give birth to it. It must have been dead for a while because it had been eaten away by maggots, and the hind was in her death throes, so I ended it for her as soon as I could.

Sometimes you do get mothers giving birth to a stillborn calf and they'll stay with it and nuzzle it and clean it and keep trying to move it. If you think animals don't have feelings, the sad sight of a mother fussing over a dead fawn or calf will convince you otherwise.

People sometimes ask me if I see many births, but I've

seen only six in my thirty years here, and those were by pure chance. I happened to be in the right place at the right time, but mostly they hide away out of sight of humans. When I first came here there were lots of situations where a calf got stuck with one front leg in and one out, so we pulled them out. Sometimes I saw them with their backsides hanging out after they'd turned round in the birth canal, and they were dead, so you needed to get them out. We would use a dart gun to put the mother to sleep and then pull the baby out by tying baler twine round the legs, because they're wet and slippery and you can't get a grip on them otherwise. Then we'd bring the mum round with a shot of Revivon and she'd spend some time licking it off; eventually she'd wander off knowing it was dead and we'd take it away.

This can be a difficult period for the new-borns for a variety of reasons, and I have a poignant memory attached to this time, which involved being called out for a dead doe. When I got there it was obvious that she'd been there for some while as her skeleton was already showing through and lying next to her was a tiny fawn skeleton. It turned out that the mother had been hit by a car and the fawn had stayed with her because she represented safety as well as food.

I remember that Dave Smith got called out for a hind that had been hit by a car in the early part of June and killed outright. But the calf, who was just hours old, was standing beside her not knowing what to do, probably thinking, There's Mum; I can smell Mum so I'm safe. Dave picked it up and his wife Debbie, whom he'd taken with him, had the poor little thing on her lap. Dave phoned Brownie and said, 'What do I do – bottle or bullet?' And Brownie said, 'I'll leave it up to you.'

Dave thought, it's easy to kill something, but to keep it alive takes a bit more effort. So he decided to give it a go. He went to the vet and explained what had happened and got some bottles of milk and teats. Then he said to Debbie that he'd give it twenty-four hours and, if it hadn't taken to the bottle by then, he would have to take it out. Young deer usually won't take to the bottle and this one seemed to be no exception. However, Debbie came downstairs the next morning in her dressing gown and held the bottle out. The calf went straight to it. After that it was plain sailing and she carried on feeding from the bottle without any problem.

However, that experience made the young deer what you might call brainwashed because, when she got older, she thought she was a human. The trouble was that she kept running up to people. She didn't want to hurt them: she just wanted to be near them. We kept putting her in the paddock but someone would leave the gate open and she'd be charging off across the park scaring people. Anyway, when she reached four years old, we decided we had no option but to take her out. It was sad but for safety reasons we couldn't let her carry on the way she was. At least she had four years of life she wouldn't have had otherwise.

One year during my early days in the park, Dave and I

came across a lot of hinds with young hanging out of their back ends. Some were dead and others were alive, and in most cases the hinds managed to eject them, although people didn't help the situation by forcing them to move on when they were trying to see what the animal was doing. So we did a lot of darting that year and, when the hind would go down and sleep, we'd pull the calf out, and revive the hind.

POST-CALVING – JUNE AND JULY

Richmond has always had a programme of ear tagging, which begins around this time of year. We tag the young deer with a different colour every year, but in order to do that we have to find them, which isn't at all easy and is very time-consuming. It involves walking through bracken until we find one, tagging it with its sex and the date and place it was found, and then, hopefully, moving on to the next one. Last year we searched every morning for six weeks and found only two, which shows how difficult it is. We do this for ageing purposes because deer are very difficult to age. The only accurate way is to tag them at birth or pull out a tooth, cut it in half, and count the rings under a microscope, like you would with a tree.

Way back in 1969 a woman named Norma Chapman ear-tagged some deer in Richmond Park for study purposes and she tagged a red hind calf. Norma was an authority on deer and wrote several books on them with her husband. When the hind eventually died she came and took the carcass away and sent me photographs of the skeleton, which showed things such as the arthritis in her spine and knees. It was really interesting to see. The hind had all her teeth with no wear and tear and she'd died of a heart attack.

Anyway, when I got the job at Richmond this hind was still alive and was hand tame, and the armed-police section at Thatched House Lodge, where Princess Alexandra lived (and still does), used to bring in all sorts of lovely goodies for her to eat, such as apples, pears and carrots, so she would always be hanging around the Lodge. They used to put the food down in a dustbin lid outside the Lodge and when the cull came around we would ask the police to paint a bright colour over her fur so that we would know who she was and wouldn't shoot her. This went on until she reached the old age of twenty-seven years and six months. Apparently we missed the record for the oldest captive deer by six months.

While she was alive she was a lovely delicate animal to feed by hand and would often come up to me if I had a carrot. If I was doing the deer feed, she would run behind the Land Rover with her head stuck in the back, with me trying to trickle the feed out. I have a photo somewhere of her with the very last calf she ever bore and in the picture is the hind herself, that year's calf and the calf from the previous year, so three generations of the old girl. When you looked at her, no way did she look twenty-seven. At a guess, you would say about seven or maybe eight.

With the males it's different. As they get older and older there are signs, such as their antlers growing back with one side deformed, while the other is still beautiful; or their teeth starting to decay; or their ability to ruminate degrading. That tells you that they've had their time and you need to take them out.

There were occasions when we'd find a young one and do everything we needed to for recording purposes, then go to release it and the silly thing would follow me to the extent that I would have to run like the clappers to get away from it. From the calf's point of view, I was Mum. Another time I remember tagging a little fallow buck and it was the only deer we managed to tag all that year. It was run over a month later and killed by a police car.

Around this time of year we get a few new-born deer handed in at reception by members of the public. Our first red calf of 2016 was found on the side of the road near the Flying Field at Sheen. This calf, which had been ear-tagged, had been handled three times throughout the course of the day, which meant there was a good chance that the mother would reject it if it smelled strongly of human scent. We let it go and we never knew if it stayed alive or died. We found another calf two weeks later on the side of the road near Ham Cross. What we did was pick it up and move it further into the bracken away from the roadside and prying eyes.

September is the month the venison house is prepared,

so it's ready for the cull. The original venison house is still *in situ* at Holly Lodge, and it is a listed building, but it's now used as the heavy horses' tack room instead of a venison house. Dave Smith, whom I worked with when I first started, said it had a soil floor and each year it would be dug out and replaced with new soil. He could remember Mr Wonham, the gamekeeper, gutting a deer while it was lying on the floor. By the time I got here it had been modernised and had a new quarry-tile floor with all the mod cons.

The trouble with the old venison house was that each animal had to be manhandled several times in order to process it, which well and truly went outside health and safety regulations. It needed five men to drag the carcass – a big one might weigh over 500 pounds – to the trailer. Then it had to be offloaded onto a bench and winched up, which was all done by hand, and finally a gambrel had to be inserted between its legs to keep them apart and enable it to be hung up. Quite a carry-on compared with today's more efficient way of doing things. So it was decided to buy another house entirely and Dave and an assistant superintendent went to Scotland to see a container venison house that was destined for the Middle East. It was one where the animal walked in one end and came out the other end in little parcels with the prices written on them, ready for the shops.

Well, they ended up buying half of it, as it was too long to fit where we wanted it to be. It came down from Scotland, was put into place standing high up on legs, and it was ready to go because it had all the necessary things already inside to do the job of cleaning the animals. It needed only to be plumbed in and have the electrics sorted out. The difference with this new house was immediately obvious. We had to handle the carcass only once as opposed to six times and it was so much easier to clean the animals. However, we were told that it would last only ten years and that was exactly how long it lasted: being a metal box meant it was only a matter of time before it rusted away. The department then spent a fortune building the new one. In this current house, the carcass isn't handled at all. It's all done by winch and cleaning the animals is even easier. It's state-of-the-art in terms of venison houses and it will see everybody out. Our vet, Peter Green, always calls it the Buckingham Palace of venison houses, and he sees a lot of them, believe me.

The stags and bucks are all in clean antler now and are just in the process of splitting up ready for the rut in the next couple of weeks. I have to say some of them are looking magnificent. The yearly cycle is gruelling – for man and beast – but, as I hope and believe the park's millions of annual visitors would agree, the results are worth the toil.

CHAPTER FIVE

What Could Possibly Go Wrong?

Attempting to keep a herd of deer six-hundred-strong safe in the environs of an urban park is, ultimately, an accident – or rather many accidents – waiting to happen. For the keepers, it's all in a day's work. At Richmond there are obviously frequent losses to accidents. In my early years there was a callout system, which was difficult to get used to because you did a total of six months on call every year. This meant that you couldn't have a normal life outside the park – going to a restaurant or cinema with your partner or going out for a drink – in case you received a call for help. It could be hard going when I was stuck in the park nonstop for weeks on end, with Maggie wanting me to go out somewhere. It was just something you had to get used to because animals are twenty-four seven, not just Monday to Friday, nine to five. The longest stint I did was thirty-five days nonstop, so it was nearly six weeks of solid working without a break. That got gritty, I can tell you. I started going stir crazy.

There was a period when I first came during which you weren't allowed to leave the park unless you had authorisation – and, anyway, there was no need because everything you required for work purposes could be drawn from the storeroom. For instance, things such as petrol, bullets, clothing, tools and materials all came from the stores, so once you came in through the gate you stayed until going-home time. Sometimes, Dave and I wouldn't leave the park for a week because not only did we work there but lived there. Dave told me once that when he first came there back in the early seventies, he had to take a member of staff out of the park to get some protective clothing and they got caught at the railway crossing at Sheen. This guy he was taking out had never seen a train before, even though he was a man in his forties. Apparently, he was born and had lived in the park and worked there as well, and obviously had never been out anywhere to see a train, which just shows how institutionalised you can become.

Even now there are times when I can go a whole week or more without leaving the park, and one thing this does is to make you more protective of the park, since it is, in effect, your world. Unlike most people who get in their cars or catch a train to go home at the end of the day, I'm already home. But there have also been times when I have been called out every day, especially when deer escaped from the park in the early years, and so I spent the whole day outside the park. Today this doesn't happen because, if a deer escapes from the park, it is no longer a Royal Parks animal. If a deer escaped today, the police would be responsible for dealing with it.

Fortunately, I have never really been in any seriously dangerous situations with deer, because if I ever felt at all threatened by an animal that was injured or writhing around on the floor, I would just shoot it first, taking away any chance of being hurt myself. You'd be amazed how powerful deer are when they are in trouble, such as when they're involved in a car accident. You can't manhandle these creatures – they're too strong, all muscle. After shooting a deer a sick or injured deer, I would then take it off the cull figure that I needed for that particular session of culling.

For all the care I took, there was one occasion when I was walking my dogs, plus Dave Smith's, and didn't notice that a stag was charging me from behind; this was in the middle of the rut, so they were all fired up. I must say that I nearly wet my pants and my reaction was to scream at the stag. I think he must have been terrified himself by my deeply humiliating shrieks, because he ran off, thank God! That was the nearest I have come to being in real danger from a deer.

I also remember an occasion when Dave and I were called out for a young stag that had got himself stuck between two layers of fencing at Pen Ponds plantation. Dave had gone in behind it to push it out the other end when suddenly it reared up on its hind legs, turned to face Dave and charged him. I thought he was a goner, but he crouched down, held his walking stick out in front of him and hit the stag right between the eyes. It was stunned for a few seconds, just enough for Dave to get out of the way. I couldn't believe how he escaped. Talk about lucky! Those were about the only times either of us ever came close to anything really dangerous.

A couple of years later, there was a sad end for one of the 'new' stags we had bought in from Norfolk , which we only discovered as the result of a callout. The younger of our two Norfolk stags was a really handsome boy. I was looking at him one day and saying what a magnificent animal he was going to make as he got older, and that quite possibly he would be our best-looking stag ever in Richmond. Then, in a bizarre turn of events, I took a callout for a dead stag the next morning and when I got there it was the same Norfolk stag. He'd been fighting and somehow got one side of his antlers trapped under the bottom wire in Prince Charles's Spinney; he couldn't get out to defend himself and was killed by the other stag. You know that this sort of thing will happen, but I couldn't believe it as I'd been talking about him only the day before.

It's usual to get callouts for a dead or injured deer during the rut – between October and December. During this time we often get called for a dead one after it's been fighting. When you have a dozen spears on top of your head, it's inevitable that one of them is going to stick in somewhere when you're going at it like the stags do.

You can also get called out for some pretty silly reasons. Once I was called for a young sorrel buck (that's one about three years old), who had somehow managed to get a Sainsbury's orange plastic bag hooked around his antlers. Every time he moved his head into the wind this bag inflated with a popping sound which spooked the entire herd at Sheen, and spooked this silly buck as well. What happened was that every time the wind caught the bag, the whole herd would run like the clappers and then the buck, wanting to be with them, would run after them making them all run even farther away. It was a nightmare and there was nothing I could do. It was getting dark, so I left it until the next morning, but by then he must have got rid of it because, when I went out the next day, none of them had a bag on his head.

I remember once I was called out for a deer, in midwinter, when it was pitch dark and I was told to get down to Palewell Common, which lies just outside the park near Sheen Gate. Apparently, one of our deer was there and the police had already arrived. I'd been in the job for only about five months, so it was one of my first times outside the park with a gun. I took what guns I thought I'd need: a shotgun and a big .243 rifle in case I had to do a heart shot; I also took a .22 in case it was lying on the floor, because you don't know what you're going to find.

Anyway, I got there and there were coppers everywhere, blue lights flashing and panda cars all over the place. An inspector came up to me and said, 'Right, where do you want my men?' And I thought, Hang on a minute, I'm only a flipping gamekeeper in the park. So I told him they could all go home. He seemed confused but I told him, 'You don't really think the deer's still here with you lot all walking round the woods with torches and blue flashing lights, do you? He's probably down in Southampton by now. You're wasting your time.' So they all got back in their panda cars and drove off and I was thinking, Thanks a lot. You've got me out of bed for nothing.

Another time I remember being called out for a deer that was in someone's garden in Sheen. The house owner said, 'That's one of your deer,' and I replied, 'No, it isn't. It's a roe deer and we don't have roe deer in the park – we've only got fallow and red deer.' And the guy said, 'Well, whose is it, then?' So I replied, 'It's wild. While it's in your garden it's nobody's, but if I shoot it, legally it belongs to you, because it only belongs to someone when it's dead, and then it belongs to the person whose land it died on.'

There have been occasions when I've had to get all the keepers together with their dogs to try to get deer out of Pembroke Gardens at Richmond. That's happened a dozen times over the years, and it's a nightmare, because deer will never go away from you. They will always try to find a gap round you to get behind. At Pembroke, the gardens taper from wide at one end down to just a few feet at the other with a gate, so, provided we all walk in a line with the dogs, the deer will go out through opened gates.

Sometimes the deer would win and we might have to

restart the process four or five times before we succeeded. And bear in mind that this has to be done very early in the morning before the public come in and mess it all up by wanting to go through the gardens for a walk. There was one occasion when we had to get all personnel in Richmond Park, including the police, to walk in a line and beat to get the deer out of Isabella Plantation. That was difficult because we really needed about a thousand people. The gardens are so wide in places, and there are so many places the deer could hide, that the job took a whole day, but we managed it in the end.

I've had to do the same thing on the golf course when someone has left the gate open all night. It was before the cattle grid went in and we had two hundred red deer on there. We had to take about two hundred yards of fencing down in order to get them out. I remember Dave Smith telling me once that he watched fallow bucks tiptoeing across a cattle grid at Pembroke and he said that you wouldn't believe what these animals can do. Mind you, the poles in the grid were square, not round, but, even so, they are clever.

We had two callouts in April 2016 to shoot a couple of bucks. The first one happened when I was on leave and Tony got called for a buck that kept falling over. It obviously had a spine problem, which was most probably the result of being hit by a car. The car driver often just drives off and leaves them like that. I think they're frightened they're going to be prosecuted so, if there's no one around to witness what happened, they think they'll just disappear as quickly as they can. The poor deer carries on running for a while, but he can't keep it up because he's so badly injured.

I've seen them like that and it's a pitiful sight. They go to stand up and then fall over; then they try again and the same thing happens. They have movement but because the spine has been snapped they can't stay on their feet. You can't leave a deer like that because the first dog that comes along will tear it to pieces. And you can't take it to the vet because it would literally cost thousands, so the only humane thing to do is take it out as quickly and cleanly as you can, so there's minimal stress and strain on the animal. Then you record it as one of the animals you have to take off your cull list, so you had, say, fifty bucks to shoot, you've now only got forty-nine.

The second incident was a buck that we'd been called out for a few times, but it took us a couple of weeks to find him. He had a large growth on his nose, which looked sore and was bleeding. We thought it was an abscess but after we shot him we discovered it wasn't, so we kept the part in the freezer to show the vet when he came. It was probably something quite harmless, but it could have been something sinister or contagious such as tuberculosis or another notifiable disease, so we had to get in touch with DEFRA. For the welfare of the herd you can't take any chances. I checked all his insides and he was fine internally, so I sent him to market.

There were no real troubles with the deer in the last couple of months of my tenure, thankfully. We had calls, but they've all turned out to be nothing of any consequence. We did have a few stags that needed to be taken out before they go to rut at the end of the month because they had broken antlers and posed a dangerous problem for other stags when fighting. If we were not careful they would end up killing a nicer stag in the process. So we took these animals out early one morning and sent them to market. One of them looked like a unicorn with one big spike and the others were older stags that had snapped one side of their antlers, which means they wouldn't be able to fight a fair fight.

There are other risks, too – to both man and beast – when we have to tranquilise our deer. This was particularly true in years gone by, chiefly due to the drug we used to use, Immobilon – it is generally brilliant for quickly knocking out deer, but does have risks and it is simply lethal for humans. These days, we no longer use it. It's the equivalent of human anaesthetics: there's an inherent risk (which is why doctors ask you so many questions before you're anaesthetised prior to surgery), and you've got to be a qualified vet to use the drug. When I was working with Dave Smith we were crown officers and we were exempt. In fact, we were exempt from most laws – except killing people!

Immobilon is certainly astonishingly quick and efficient.

If you've got a deer that's half asleep in the sun, it'll just go over. Sometimes you only need to use 0.5cc, and when you're working in a public park, the last thing you want is a half-mad stag running around with a needle hanging out of its backside for prolonged periods of time – something I have sadly had acute experience of.

The instance occurred when the gamekeepers from Windsor Great Park came to Richmond for a team day out and to meet staff here and see how things were done compared with their own park. When he saw our herd he was gobsmacked. He said, 'How do you manage to get such good animals with night-time culling? I can't manage that with *daytime* culling.'

I told him that he could have some of ours if he wanted and he said, 'Really? But how much is that going to cost?' I said, 'I can't be seen charging Her Majesty the Queen for her own deer – she'll throw me in the Tower. So you can have them for nothing.' He couldn't believe his ears, and we agreed he could come back in March when they had all but cast their antlers (if they haven't completely cast, you have to saw them off before transporting, although it doesn't hurt the animal because it's dead bone).

Come March, the head keeper turned up and organised his men and trailers to take the animals back after they had been darted. The guy doing the darting didn't tell me at this point that he was not using Immobilon, the drug needed to knock the deer out quickly. He was using another drug altogether, one that was much slower to act. So the first animal he darted got up and ran off at full speed across the park with us lot in hot pursuit, trying to keep an eye on the dart in case it fell out.

We eventually caught up with it – it was still very much awake and was taking ages to go over. It was at this point that I questioned him to discover he wasn't using Immobilon. So I said, 'For goodness' sake, throw that stuff away and use only Immobilon otherwise we're packing up. I can't have animals running wild with darts hanging out of their arses with the public all around. I've got to have the animals on the floor in moments. This isn't a bloody zoo.' He changed the drug, and the next animal fell where it was darted and we were able to get it into a box trailer and on its way back to Windsor within minutes. Once the animal is in the trailer you can inject a drug called Revivon, which brings it round in seconds. You want the animal standing up before you start driving off. We started at about 8 a.m. and finished with the last animal at about 3 p.m., and we darted ten stags and one hind. The head keeper was well pleased, but I'm not ashamed to say my blood ran cold when that stag took off.

However, even for deer, it is not risk free. We often get call-outs when two fighting males end up locked together. I had a situation with two bucks once when I was working alongside Dave Smith, who was head keeper at that time, when we had to decide whether to shoot one or dart it. They'd been fighting all night and were literally down on their knees. But the trouble with Immobilon is that ideally you have to have them at rest. If they've been running and they're puffing and blowing you usually need three times the amount to knock them out. Immobilon is a heart relaxant and it could give them a heart attack in high doses.

Anyway, we darted one of the bucks and it dropped to the floor but, as with the Norfolk stag and his rival, they were still stuck together. So we darted the other one and, in the meantime, the first one died of a heart attack. The other was still alive and we managed to get them apart; we brought him round and he trotted off. We watched him and thought he didn't look right. Sadly, he died later that day.

And as for Immobilon's potential risks for humans? The fact is, one cc of Immobilon can be lethal in the wrong hands. When the person doing the darting is aiming the dart gun, everyone is watching for where the dart might fall. If he misses and a member of the public picks it up . . . Well, it's best not to go there! If the tiniest bit splashes onto your skin, you've only got seconds. If you don't get the Narcon into you quickly, you are a goner (Narcon is the human equivalent of Revivon, to bring you back round if you were unfortunate enough to be affected by Immobilon). If you put just 1cc into a water system, it would kill hundreds. When you were using it you had to suit up like a spaceman.

You also have to use a different drug if you want your deer to remain fit for human consumption. If one has been darted and it's come to the end of its breeding life, you have to incinerate the whole carcass because the drug stays in the large muscles of the body and it's absolutely lethal to humans in more ways than one. Also, if a fox or a badger ate any of the carcass, it would be in trouble too. So the Department for Environment, Food and Rural Affairs (DEFRA) sends special metal ear tags with the transport licence that are all numbered specifically to you and the animals you're darting.

Beyond the obvious safety issues, this really is not nearly as easy as it looks. The dart gun is a nightmare to use because it's so inaccurate – you never know where it's going to land. When you see them on the TV darting hippos from a helicopter they show only the one shot that knocks them down and they look like crack shots who never miss. They don't show you the three previous months when they've taken thousands of shots and missed with every one!

CHAPTER SIX

The Silliest
Animal of All

The greatest (perhaps only) of Richmond Park's faults is, sadly, an inevitable one. Namely, it is a public space. Walkers, as well as motorists and cyclists, have rights of access, and the Park receives about five and a half million visits per year. If I had to sum up everything about my role, it would be to say that balancing the needs of the deer with the demands of the visitors underpins everything I do. I often say that the deer are OK – they can look after themselves if left to their own devices. The problem is usually what I call the silliest animal that's ever walked the planet – humans.

But they're not all silly, so I'll kick off with an account of some of my good human contacts. Multitasking comes with the territory of my job. I have to be a public relations officer, liaising with journalists on news stories and topical issues. I'm a teacher, educating members of the public about the park, and I also have to lecture students about deer management. I remember working with a young Californian student named Megan, who came over to England four years running to carry out behavioural studies with deer. She'd stay locally and come up to the park every day to observe and record the deer. After spending time with us she'd go on to France, where the rut is later than in England, and then she'd fly out to New Zealand, where the rut takes place even later in the year. I told her that I'd love to see a copy of her thesis, but I never heard from her again, which was sad.

It was different story with a young English student named Katie, whose mother wrote to me to say that Katie was hoping to go to college to do a veterinary degree. Katie asked if she could come up and speak to me, which I was happy to agree to. The two of them made several visits to the park, travelling all the way across London from their home near Greenwich. They came up for the culls and I let Katie see the dead animals, with their viscera ready for her to examine. I explained to her about various diseases and showed her where the major organs were and other stuff, and she took samples home with her – eyeballs, bits of lung, you name it!

After their visits had finished – and I'd accumulated a cupboard full of tins of biscuits, which they brought me every time they came – I received a letter from Katie's mum telling me that she'd been trying to get a place at Liverpool College, to train as a vet. They took on only four students a year for that particular course, but her mother told me that Katie had been offered a place purely on the strength of her time spent studying with me in the park, which was good to hear.

One of my main occupations though, sadly, is acting as the park's 'dustpan and broom' – which mostly involves clearing up blood and guts, usually after humans have done silly things. I'm not a man who's squeamish or scares easily, but there have been times in my job when even I have had to look away after animals have sustained severe injuries. Sometimes it makes the hairs on the back of your neck stand up. This is when I also have to assume another major role, that of world-class diplomat. For example, when a deer is knocked down by a car and you see a woman standing there crying her eyes out, the last thing they want is to see you coming along with your gun to put the animal out of its misery.

There have been many incidents during the time I've been here in which cars have hit deer. I've had them under the car and inside the car when they've gone through the windscreen. Mostly they're alive and need dispatching, which is scary in itself because, when you pull that trigger, you hope the injured deer drops in one go, rather than dying slowly and in pain. I used to smoke years ago and rolled my own cigarettes, but I have sometimes had to sit on my hands to try to calm down because they would shake so much after I had put down an animal that I would spill all my tobacco.

One such incident involved a dog chasing a master stag – a big boy. This one ran straight into an oncoming car, a tiny little hatchback. When I got there the paramedics were working on two unconscious people in the road. The car was a write-off and the stag was a short distance away with a busted back leg with the bone showing through and lacerations the entire length of its body. It also had a broken antler that was covered in velvet (a temporary membrane when the antler is forming), and when this happens they can bleed to death because there are major arteries running through them. It was writhing around on the floor, knowing, I think, what was to come, so I had to make sure I dispatched it quickly.

I remember Dave telling me about a horrific incident that happened in April twenty years ago when a herd of red hinds were crossing the road by Sawyer's Wood and a car went straight through the middle of them. When he got there it was like a war zone with bodies everywhere, some dead and some still alive. It turned out that four were dead and three had to be followed up and shot because they had broken legs and cuts on their bodies. I always say that if you knock down a red deer, you're not looking where you're going, because reds have road sense, unlike fallow, which just bolt across. Anyway, the woman who mowed down this lot claimed she didn't see them until the last minute, which was obviously

THE SILLIEST ANIMAL OF ALL

bending the truth, to say the least. I make no excuses for repeating myself: we are the only species on earth that causes such suffering. If I had my way, I'd ban all cars and dogs from the park, but that's about as likely to happen as my becoming prime minister.

Another incident that's etched on my memory was when I got called out for a fallow buck that had been hit by a car at the bottom of Broomfield Hill, which is a very steep incline. The traffic was backed up all the way to my lodge at Kingston Gate, so I had to drive off-road all the way to the bottom of the hill. When I arrived there I saw a crowd of about fifty people huddled together in the middle of the road. Then, as I approached, I saw that the man and woman who'd knocked the deer down had got a blanket from the car and were cradling the buck's head in their laps. I asked everyone to move back slowly and told them that I would have to dispatch it, the reason being that if you can touch these animals, you know they're in serious trouble, because usually they hate being handled. I said that you couldn't see the injuries internally and that if you took off its fur coat you would probably see that it had broken all its ribs, punctured its lungs and spleen, and more.

The people watching were saying things like, 'Oh no, he's going to shoot it,' but they backed off and I didn't have any trouble. In the end, I couldn't move it because it turned out to have shattered its spine, so I had to shoot it in the road. Sometimes you have to be quite firm with people, as they just don't understand what needs to be done. I'll say something like, 'No photographs, please. This isn't a cabaret act. All you're going to see is a lovely animal that has to be destroyed.' And I put it out of its misery as fast as I can.

In contrast, one can sometimes be seen as a bit of a hero rather than a villain. I was called out one day during winter when there was a thick sheet of ice covering Pen Ponds, and a doe had fallen through the ice after being chased by a dog, who'd singled her out from the herd. She ran across the ice because she wanted to get to the island in the middle of the pond, where she obviously thought she'd be safe from her pursuer. When I arrived on the scene there was a group of about ten people waiting to see what I was going to do. The dog had long since disappeared, and I went to get a boat and row out through the ice to see if I could get to the doe. However, as soon as I got to her I could tell she wouldn't survive because she was cold to her core. Anyway, I gave it a go, but it was a devil of a job rowing through the ice with one arm, using my other arm to keep the doe's head above water.

I managed to get her back to the bank and the people stood there clapping me. Some women in the group put their coats over the deer and started rubbing her, which I encouraged, and they did so for about an hour. I could tell she wouldn't pull through and I said to the women that the only possible chance she had was if she could be soaked in a bath of warm water, and that just wasn't possible. It was getting dark, and I told them that if I left the doe there, the first fox that came along would start tearing at her while she was still alive, and therefore the only solution was to dispatch her. I would usually have shot her in the water, but at least this way the people could see that I'd done everything possible to try to save her, which would help to dispel the idea that we're just murderers, which certain members of the public believe. In this case, they were understanding and supportive, but tongues will wag, and you never know what people will say about you behind your back.

There's one more role this job demands, which can be equally stressful in its way: acting as a potential witness in court cases. There have been occasions in my career when I have been called to stand by for a court appearance as a crown witness in wildlife crime. When I took on the job this was a completely new experience for me and I found the first time quite a worry, as until then I'd never seen the inside of a courtroom, let alone acted as a witness in connection with doing my job.

The first time I was called happened when I hadn't been working in the park very long. At about eleven o'clock one Sunday morning, two old boys, both in their seventies, were caught poaching with ferrets. What possessed them to do it in the heat of summer and in such an open park is beyond me. I was called to confirm what they had been doing, and the police confiscated all their nets, bags and rabbits as evidence that I had to hold. I had to keep the rabbits in the deep freeze. When it went to court I was lucky, because the pair pleaded guilty and I was told to stand down. I was relieved because acting as a witness was not something I'd expected to be doing when I came here and it hadn't been explained to me at the interview stage.

Another time, the police made contact with Dave and me and explained that they had been called to a back garden shed that had a bad smell coming from it. They warned us that they weren't sure whether it was human body parts all chopped up in buckets or a deer, and they asked us if we would be prepared to go and have a look to confirm one way or another. As we were used to seeing the body parts of animals, we said OK. Much to our relief it did turn out to be one of our deer that this guy had poached, cut up and put in buckets. The trouble was that he did this in July, when it was really hot, so the buckets were crawling with maggots and the deer flesh was starting to putrefy. I hasten to add that he was nicked.

There have been numerous dog attacks for which I've been asked to get ready to appear. One incident concerned a woman who was walking her dog when it chased a fallow doe and mauled it to death. It actually died as I arrived there. Again, I was lucky, because she pleaded guilty and I didn't have to appear. She was fined £120 with court costs, so it proved to be an expensive afternoon walking her dog.

Another memory is of a woman whose dog chased a stag across the park and caused to it run straight into an oncoming car, nearly killing both occupants. I was called out to shoot the deer and write up what damage was done. She was taken to court, where she was found guilty, fined £1,200 pounds and ordered to pay court costs. This was on top of what we were going to charge her for the cost of my time and the animal, which in the end we decided not to pursue. There have been dozens of times when this sort of thing has happened, but each time I've been lucky that the people accused have pleaded guilty. So far I haven't actually had to appear in court in thirty years of working here.

There was one incident that made me laugh even though I know I shouldn't have found it funny, really. This woman's Alsatian was chasing a herd of hinds and I was in hot pursuit with the police as they were coming up to Ham Cross, heading for Ham Gate. The herd went to cross the road and there was this little old Morris Minor with a soft top coming down the hill with a learner driver at the wheel. All of sudden the deer started to jump over her car and one went straight through the soft roof into the back seat. The driver careered off the road into a tree with this deer sitting on the back seat. It did look funny at the time. Luckily, the deer was not injured and no one was hurt. The dog owner was taken to court and found guilty in her absence as she had fled to Spain to escape punishment. Apparently, she had been walking the dog for a friend who was on holiday. We never found out if she came back to face the music.

My worst case came in the 1990s, when one morning in mid-April I found a dead badger, a sow in milk. We sent it off for an autopsy and when the report came back it stated that its back had been broken by a blunt instrument and it had been savaged by dogs. Alarm bells started ringing everywhere and the next step was to get the police involved. A few days passed and another dead badger showed up with exactly the same injuries. A sergeant in the park police got onto the West Country badger group, and Operation Brock was started, which involved groups of twenty people taking turns to stay out all night seven nights a week to see if we could catch whoever it was. There were more than three hundred people involved in the operation altogether.

In the end, whoever it was had killed twenty-two badgers, all sows in milk, during April, May and June. Not only had they killed the sows, but all the cubs, too, because they would still have been on milk. They also almost completely killed off some setts that were years old. In fact, in 2015, the setts had only just recovered to the same level as they had been before all this trouble began, way back in the nineties, so they have taken a long time to return to normal. The culprits were never caught and they stopped that year. Whether they were locked up for some other crime I don't know, but, thankfully, they never came back. However, in those three short, grisly months they did a lot of damage to the badger population of the park.

But people are more often plain ignorant rather than villainous. They naturally want to get up close and personal with the deer. They're athletic and graceful and they can be drop-dead gorgeous, especially the saucer-eyed fawns and calves. They offer children – and adults – a rare opportunity to connect with nature at its most appeal-ing. That's why so many of them travel from every corner of the world to this oasis of green so close to London that forms the largest enclosed park in Europe, as big as all the other seven royal parks combined and three times the size of New York's Central Park. But the deer are not Disney cartoon characters: they're wild, unpredictable creatures, and it's all too easy to forget that.

It's when 'up close' becomes 'too close' that I draw the line, not because I want to deprive deer lovers of their chance to share a quick selfie with the stags, but because I know only too well the potential for disaster and how vital it is to understand the reality of the situation. People are led into a false sense of security: because they can walk through a herd and get very close they assume the deer are tame. But they are not. They don't feel the same love for us that we do for them. They don't like getting too close to humans, they don't like being touched, and if someone has a dog that starts barking at them, they'll react. The bottom line is that the deer tolerate us, but that's as far as it goes.

Even though, strictly speaking, the deer in Richmond Park are in captivity within the park walls, they go through all the same feelings and emotions as the wild deer of Scotland do. To a great extent, they look after themselves all year round, and Tony and I are here to keep an eye out for when it all goes wrong. And, sadly, it often does, with the fault far more often than not lying with the two-legged species.

I'm still amazed by the risks people take when they spot the chance to sneak that intimate close-up, with or without a camera. They ignore the signs of a deer's unease, and in some cases they're so determined to become amateur David Attenboroughs that they're almost literally in the deer's faces. Then they seem mystified or upset when that 'docile' creature decides enough is enough. It's not only deer that get injured, sometimes fatally: it also happens to dogs that get too cocky for their own good. And people get hurt, too, occasionally quite seriously, especially during the rut, when hormones are running wild and when deer perceive humans as intruders and threats. And, of course, when it comes to protecting their young, they take no prisoners. If you see a hind with a newborn, no matter how tempting it is to capture the 'Aah!' factor on film, the watchword is: 'Don't!' If that baby bleats you'll have twenty hinds around you and the mother will follow you all the way to the gate.

Many times I've had to warn people to back off before

they are attacked. I once found a guy standing between two stags fighting. They were ten feet apart and he was right in the middle of them in the wide-open space of the Flying Field at Sheen. How long he'd been there I don't know, but he was one lucky so-and-so. I warned him to move away, and when he assured me he knew what he was doing as he'd been photographing them for twenty-five years, I gently advised him not to be such a fool. When he refused to cooperate I told him that if he didn't get out of there fast I'd have a copper on him. I once told a woman that she wouldn't walk so close to a tiger, so why with a deer? After all, they have a dozen spear points sitting on their heads. These guys can put holes in places where you didn't know you could have them. I've seen them dig two-foot holes in the ground with their antlers, so it's no good lying on the floor. And you certainly won't outrun them: they're like gazelles. They can do 0–30 mph in seconds.

During my first May working in the park in 1987, I had to deal with two incidents involving dogs and hinds on the same day. I had a bleeper then and I got called out nine times in twenty minutes; I was thinking, hang on, I haven't done the first one yet. Give us a chance! Anyway, I made my way down towards Ham for the first callout and I saw this woman wearing orange trousers, and holding a dog. She had about thirty hinds all around her and they were all about to run towards her and kick her. She was crying her eyes out and she was so frightened that she had wet herself.

The dog hadn't attacked the hinds but he didn't need

to, because, with the young being born at this time of year, the hinds will attack any dog that comes near. They don't care if it's a tiny little thing or a huge great beast, they see it as a threat to their young and they think, I'll have you! Anyway, I got this woman to the car park at Pembroke Lodge and into her car and she was still really distraught but basically OK, and she'd certainly learned her lesson After I left her, I drove back towards Ham, where I'd found her, and, blow me, there was a guy doing exactly the same thing in exactly the same spot surrounded by hinds.

Hinds obviously don't have antlers, so they attack with their feet, which have two slots. These slots at the front of the foot turn inwards and they're like razors. We had a guy here once who was hit by a hind down his thigh and it opened his leg up from his hip to his knee. He was rushed to hospital by the police. The hinds will either lash out with their back legs like a horse or stand up and use their front legs to box you. But they're only doing what any mother would do if she felt her young were being threatened. And you have to remember that these deer are being chased by dogs all year round, so as soon as they see one they automatically register a threat.

I don't know why, but that weekend I had a lot of hinds walking around with calves half in and half out. I think it had something to do with the fact that, once the public see the calf coming out of the back end, they want to see it actually being born and they keep moving the hind on. So, instead of her just being relaxed and lying down and pushing to get her baby out, she has to keep moving. That really shows you just how difficult Joe Public is – they just won't leave the deer alone. They're like flies round a cow's backside.

Another thing that people don't realise is that by getting involved so stupidly, they're interfering with the natural behaviour and habits of the deer, in this case the breeding process. They're fighting because they're trying to keep their harem, and if people get too close and the hinds all run off, the stags are fighting for nothing. I recently had a woman trying to feed grass to a big stag near Richmond Gate. I had to shout to her and tell her not to feed the deer. I told her that she wasn't just in breach of a by-law, it was also extremely dangerous. Then, minutes after that episode, I spotted two big bucks on the side of the road with three people approaching them from one direction, another three from a different direction and a third group of three coming at them from another. They couldn't understand that those deer had nowhere to go except into the busy road.

The public also don't realise that if they get to touch a baby deer it can be fatal to that animal. What happens is that the young deer picks up the scent of the human who's doing the touching – whether it's perfume, deodorant, aftershave or whatever – and when the mother comes back she rejects it. The mum is its food-giver and its thirst-quencher, so that's basically writing its death warrant.

Bizarrely, people also seem to view Richmond Park as some sort of idyllic dumping ground for unwanted animals. Over my thirty years of working here at Richmond, I have come across all manner of animals that have been released into the park by the public, many of them unwanted pets. The sad thing is that these people think they are doing them a favour by letting them go into the wild here in the park, when in reality they have as good as condemned them to a horrible death. That's because most of the animals that I have come across didn't know what a predator was or where to get food or water. In many cases they wouldn't even last a day.

I hadn't been here long when Dave and I got a call saying that there were two very large squirrels near Sheen Gate. When we got there we discovered that they were in fact chinchillas, which do look a little like giant squirrels. As luck would have it, they were friendly and we were able to pick them up and put them in boxes. We contacted a children's petting farm in London and they came and collected the chinchillas, so that episode had a happy ending.

Dave was called out one Sunday morning to deal with what he was told was a six-foot-long orange snake in Isabella Plantation. When he arrived there, the RPC sergeant, Nick Bryant, was there and sure enough there was a bright orange snake about six feet long. Nick told Dave to pick it up while he held the sack. So Dave said, 'You pick it up and I'll hold the sack.' Nick said, 'It's all right, it won't bite.' So Dave said, 'You won't mind picking it up, then.' Between them, they eventually somehow managed to get the snake into the sack. Meanwhile, London Zoo had been called and when their people arrived they said the snake wasn't dangerous. They identified it as an American corn snake. What on earth the people who let it go were thinking I haven't a clue. Just its colour alone was enough to make it prey for every predator in the park.

On another occasion, I was in my greenhouse at home when a black gerbil hopped into the house and proceeded to nibble scraps on the floor. At this stage I wasn't too concerned, but when I went back indoors the gerbil hopped into my front room. I thought, I don't want this thing indoors nesting where I can't find it. So I got up and gave chase and, luckily, it ran straight out the back door. In the end I had to build a gate with fine wire to stop it coming indoors and eventually it disappeared and didn't return.

Dave was walking the dogs late one night and, as he approached his house, he moved what he thought was a toad in the road with his walking stick so it wouldn't get squashed by a car. Suddenly this 'toad' turned and grabbed the end of his walking stick. It turned out to be a tarantula that was as big as a toad. Dave panicked and flicked it off to the side of the road. It was certainly a potential danger to the public, but there's little doubt that it wouldn't have survived the first frost. Why people have these things as pets in the first place is beyond me.

A goat once appeared in the park. It was on its last legs, all skin and bone. The couple who owned it were being taken to court for cruelty by the RSPCA and I assume they thought that, if they dumped it in Richmond Park, the court case wasn't going to happen. They were wrong: the court case did go ahead and Dave had to keep the goat as evidence. As luck would have it, the goat wasn't needed as they pleaded guilty, and Dave fell in love with the goat and decided to keep her – for eleven years. She died having enjoyed a far happier life than she might have done otherwise.

Back in 2002 I was called out because a member of the public had brought in a baby jay in a cardboard box. When I got him home I really didn't know what I was going to do with him. He was a tiny, scrawny fledgling and he did look a sorry sight. As I picked him up, lots of tiny feather mites ran over my hand and I said to my wife Maggie that he must be scratching all day long. As luck would have it, I had some spray that killed parasites, so I held the bird and Maggie sprayed him until he was dripping. I put him in an old budgie cage until the next morning, hoping he would still be alive. Sure enough, he was, but the floor of the cage was thick with dead mites. He must have been so relieved.

We decided we were going to have a go at feeding him and, surprisingly, he would eat anything we put in front of him. From then on, Maggie took over the duties of feeding and cleaning, and also named him Barney. After three or four weeks had passed and Barney had filled out, I told Maggie that we would have to let him go because he couldn't stay in a budgie cage forever. Maggie reluctantly agreed, so the following day we took the cage outside, opened the door and let him come out in his own time, which he did immediately. We thought he would fly off but instead he flew onto my shed roof and started flapping his wings the way nestlings do when they want food – Barney wanted Maggie to play Mum.

Incredibly, Barney stayed in our garden for three months and would wake us up early in the mornings by sitting on our windowsill calling for food. He became so friendly with Maggie that one day, whilst she was lying on the lawn sunbathing, Barney was lying between her legs with his wings out doing the same. Sometimes Maggie would be on all fours looking for beetles and worms and he'd be right there with her.

Alas, we went on a fortnight's holiday and when we came back he was gone. Barney did provide us with some special moments and memories, particularly for Maggie. We did have Barney for most of the summer that year, which was far more than we could have expected. I had never realised just how intelligent those birds are. And, when we last saw him, Barney was a fully grown, beautiful jay.

Of course, Joe Public don't just present a danger to the deer, or the animals they ditch here – they present a danger to themselves. Never better is this exemplified than during the culling season. Before we begin culling we have to give out notices to local newspapers, radio and other media, put flyers and posters everywhere and notices on all the gates telling pedestrians to be aware that the park is shutting. We warn them that there will be people firing guns, so it will be dangerous to enter when the gates are shut, and that if you're caught, you will be officially cautioned. In November and February the gates will have been shut to traffic before the pedestrian gates, which are shut at 8 p.m., but when I first came to the park they used to shut all the gates at the same time, 5.30 p.m., and I can remember having lots of people and lots of cars outside my house at Kingston Gate all wanting to get out. I got fed up with people knocking on my door and being out there sorting out the mess for hours, and eventually it was decided to close the pedestrian gates later.

Of course, people have a habit of ignoring what you tell them, even if it's for their own good. I've often encountered individuals walking – or, more accurately, staggering – in the park after closing time (park and pubs), not knowing what they were doing or where they were going because they were so drunk. Many of them were so far gone they were walking down the middle of the road, hardly able to stay upright. When I asked them what they were doing there, they would usually say, 'I'm on my way home.' I have had people singing and playing guitars outside my house at two in the morning and on one occasion it was so annoying that I rushed out of the house topless wielding a rake. In those days I had loads of hair, which was all over the place because I'd just got up. I must have looked like the Wild Man of Borneo. Another time, I was woken in the middle of the night by a guy outside my house, who was out of his brains and playing a clarinet. I said, 'If you don't eff off right now I'll stick that clarinet where you'll blow it permanently.'

Years ago, when Dave Smith was still head keeper and we were out culling and were driving along by Beverley Brook, I spotted a wheel in the undergrowth, which I assumed belonged to someone's bicycle. I carried on driving and almost ran over a bloke lying on the ground in front of me covered in a blanket, which had then been covered by leaves falling from the trees.

I was phoning the police to say that there was a homeless man in the park when suddenly the guy got up from under the blanket and Dave said to me, 'Look, the poor guy's got no legs.' What we had thought was a bike was a wheelchair. Anyway, the police eventually came down to sort him out and subsequently told us that he attacked them with a machete. It turned out he had done two robberies that day. He was hooked on drugs and was robbing people and attacking them with the machete to get money to feed his habit.

When I think of the changes I've noticed in the park since I've been here, I realise it's not just the deer: it's the people, too. Twenty-five years ago, I could walk from my house at Kingston Gate with my shotgun, my bags and my dogs, and I'd zigzag across the park shooting squirrels, rabbits, crows and pigeons and get to the office at Holly

Lodge on the other side of the park at 8.30 a.m. without seeing another soul. If I came out of my house now with a gun, there'd be someone ringing the police every ten minutes. Nowadays there's nonstop traffic, streams of cyclists and, of course, pedestrians.

The change was so striking that it was almost as if everyone suddenly woke up and thought, why don't I use Richmond Park? I think that was very much due to the famous 'Petersham Hole' in Petersham Road, which runs along one side of the park. The road was closed after a sewer collapsed in 1979 and the resulting hole became a part of local folklore. A local newspaper correspondent reported a sighting while he was on holiday in Spain of somebody wearing a T-shirt bearing the slogan 'I'VE SEEN THE PETERSHAM HOLE!' The repairs and disruption lasted for eighteen months, during which time eighty-four deer were killed as result of the extra traffic passing through the park, which was the only route available if you wanted to get from Kingston to Richmond or vice versa. Having seen how beautiful the park was and what it had to offer, people obviously started thinking they would use it for recreation as well as a travel route, and it's never been quite the same since.

In an ideal world, I would love to see the park shut for one day a week, with no traffic and no people whatsoever allowed in, to give the animals one twenty-four-hour period to relax and chill out. I'd like to see restrictions on people who live in the park as well. Even more controversially, I'd like to see a ban on all dogs,

Above: A fawn will lie in the bracken quietly all day while its mother forages. Unfortunately, visitors to the park may come by and touch them. If a fawn is tainted with the scent of a human encroacher, its mother will reject it, effectively signing its death warrant.

Below: I hold a tiny fawn we decided to attempt to rescue. As my good friend Dave once said, it's easy to take a life, but to save one is much harder.

Above: All creatures great and small: the park has a stunning range of flora and fauna, beyond the obvious deer. We once rescued a little owl, like this one, which had fallen injured from a tree.

Below: A stag roars to scare rivals away from his hard-won stand of females.

Hitching a ride: a fallow buck quizzically eyeballs a magpie that's landed on his rump (*above*). Meanwhile, a red hind is less attentive toward its resident flock of little interlopers.

The park is never
more beautiful
than during misty
mornings and
fiery sunsets. If it
weren't for that
spectacular London
skyline, you could
be forgiven for
thinking you were
in the open wilds of
Scotland or Wales.

Above: Red stags are astonishingly strong and brave – and incredibly fierce in the rut. It's not unheard of for a stag to break an antler in the heat of battle.

Below: Our deer feast on sweet chestnut and berries, and in doing so act as natural landscapers, maintaining that characteristic line of lower branches six feet off the ground.

Above: At work with a shotgun. One has to be incredibly careful using any firearm inside Richmond Park, as some of my rifles could easily send a bullet as far as three miles away if I take a bad shot.

Below: Snod, my faithful gun dog and closest friend. Saying goodbye to him was one of the hardest things I have ever done.

Above: A young fallow buck fiercely stares us down. . .

Below: A group of young bucks begin testing out their strength by springing up and butting each other.

Above: A stag with his antlers in the final throes of fraying. While those bloody strips and smears can look incredibly alarming to visitors, it is a totally normal process in which the blood vessels shrink and the velvet covering falls off to reveal clean antler.

Below: One of our magnificent herd of red deer, in strong body and clean antler – the pride of Richmond Park. There is no finer sight.

© *Tony Hatton*

because there would be so many benefits to the park. We had an ecologist here called Nigel Reeve who did a study of dog faeces left around the park and found, among other things, that there was on average four tons of the stuff deposited every year. What people do now is pick up their dog mess in a bag and then throw it on the ground, so now you've got litter and dog mess to deal with. And you'd be surprised how many people come to the park in cars just to walk a dog. So, if you banned dogs, you'd have no muck, fewer cars, no deer-chasing and no problems in the skylark areas, where they almost destroyed the skylark population by disturbing the nests on the ground. In reality, though, there's not a chance of that happening: there'd be a public outcry.

I remember once back in the eighties when we had a huge snowfall and the public were sliding down Petersham slopes – not just one or two people but hundreds of them. So you had about a hundred walking back up again while another hundred or so were coming down. The injury list got so bad that Kingston Hospital rang our office to say that we had to do something to control it because they had run out of doctors and beds. The problem was made worse by the fact that people weren't just whizzing down the slopes during the day, but were doing it at night as well, because it stays light when snow falls.

We even had to call in an air ambulance to pick up some guy who collided with the fence at the bottom and broke a dozen bones. After it was all over it took two men three weeks to clear an estimated nine tons of rubbish, which included car bonnets, dustbin lids, trays, anything that would slide, even road signs and sheets of metal. Imagine a sheet of metal hurtling down and hitting someone on the way up; it can do serious damage. To try to stop the heavy-metal brigade in the future we planted a line of trees in the way to make it impossible to slide down to any great length; but, if it ever snows and you come to the park at midnight, you will still see hundreds of people zooming up and down.

Then there is the potential damage park to the park itself to consider. Richmond Park is teeming with people year round, many of them parents with their children enjoying the wide-open spaces and the many natural attractions that the park has to offer. That said, Richmond is different from other major parks in terms of the restrictions it places on certain activities. These have been put in place to maintain its status as a National Nature Reserve, a Site of Special Scientific Interest and a Special Area of Conservation.

So, for example, visitors are asked not to interfere with trees or plants or take anything out of the park, such as any wood (dead wood is home to rare beetle species and other insects), fungi, deer antlers, sweet chestnuts, grasses and flowers. Indeed, we've had to put up signage telling people not to take the sweet chestnuts, as they are a big part of the deer's diet: they need them to put on bodyweight going into winter. We've had to do this because there were some years when the public filled dustbin liners so full with chestnuts that they almost weren't able to lift their bags. There were pounds of them, which would have been used in the restaurant trade. Taking away the chestnuts is no longer legal, and the same goes for the mushrooms in the park.

The public are also cautioned not to get too close to the deer (a warning that is ignored with unbelievable frequency); not to interfere with wildlife habitats, such as birds' nests (nosy dogs rooting around almost extinguished the skylark population at one point), anthills and dead wood (as above); and not to feed swans, wildfowl or any other birds. They must keep to established paths, not light a barbecue and keep dogs under control at all times (another requirement that might as well be written in invisible ink for all the notice some people take of it).

It's an interesting fact that most of the complaints received by the park management are made by users complaining about other users: dog walkers allowing dogs to get out of control and not picking up their mess; cyclists whizzing around inconsiderately; car drivers doing the same and also parking in places where they shouldn't, especially in disabled spaces. As someone once said, you can't legislate against stupidity and, without wishing to labour the point, I've already made it clear which species I think is the stupidest of all. You could put up massive notices end to end in the park warning about the dangers of approaching the deer because they're wild animals and you'd still get people sticking cameras in the stags' faces, oblivious of the risk they're running.

Anyone who ignores all the notices during the rut and comes in late at night runs a serious risk of being shot, because we can't see who's off in the distance. With the spotlight on the deer you can see only what's in the light. Three hundred yards away there could be someone crouching down and I could easily hit them. The other thing people do that's strictly against the rules is having barbecues, and we've lost quite a few veteran oaks over the years because people think they've put the ashes out and they've tipped them into a hole in the tree and burnt the tree down. If that isn't a tragedy, I don't know what is.

Admittedly, sometimes dealing with the public can be difficult for different, less blameful reasons. You have to be prepared for just about anything in this job but, even so, some of the situations you encounter can still throw you. I'll never forget one old boy, who was very smart and looked like an ex-colonel: handlebar moustache, tattersall shirt and tie, tweed jacket and cap. He was found wondering around the park aimlessly and someone asked him who he was, how old he was, where he had come from and where he was going, and he answered 'I don't know' to all of those questions. His mind was completely gone. They put his picture in the local paper, and a young couple came forward and said, 'That's our dad.' He'd been kicked out of hospital and sent home and they hadn't told his son and daughter. It was very sad, but at least it ended well.

We also had a spell during the nineties in Sidmouth Plantation when it was so thick with rhododendrons, the common *ponticum* species, that it was like the Burmese jungle, and in it we came across four or five patients with mental health issues, who had been kicked out of hospitals and institutions. The government had closed these places down and ejected many patients into the hands of 'care in the community'. These poor people had been sent out into the world with their pills and they had no idea where to go.

Anyway, this group of four of five had decided to set up home in Sidmouth and had made quite an elaborate little camp. They had made tunnels in the *ponticum* and Dave and I went through them and found that they'd made chambers with makeshift beds with tarpaulins over them. They must have been there quite a long time because there had obviously been a lot of work involved in creating their new home. Eventually, the police became involved because the *ponticum* was all being torn up and the former patients had nowhere to go.

One still has to maintain one's sense of humour, mind. Talking of the police reminds me of a story that made it on to BBC One years ago. A woman described how she was driving her car through the park when suddenly the engine started to cough and fart and go wrong. This happened near Robin Hood Gate, so she stopped and got out and was looking under the bonnet, not really knowing what to do. As she stood up from under the bonnet she was hit on the head by a duck that apparently had died in flight and crashed into her. So she said, 'I was standing there dazed with this duck in one hand holding my bloodied head in the other when one of your Royal Parks policemen turned up on a cycle, stopped and said, "Hey up, madam, you can't take that duck – it's poaching."' He grabbed the duck and rode off, leaving her there. The next day in the yard we were all in fits of laughter, but we never found out which policemen it was who ducked the issue.

CHAPTER SEVEN

The Olympics Come to Richmond

In July 2012 the Olympics came to London and the Royal Parks staged some of the events. There was beach volleyball at St James's; Greenwich held the equestrian events; and Richmond Park was part of the route for the road race in the cycling. As the UK was the host country, there was no expense spared. Tony and I had to travel into London to get a special pass that would allow us access to the cycling route if we needed it in an emergency.

We also had to take a shotgun to Greenwich in case a deer got into trouble and had to be shot while the Olympic event was taking place. We weren't allowed to carry one up there by road, because, past a certain date, there was to be a lockdown for security reasons. No one would be allowed in the zone with a gun once this lockdown was in place and we were told that, if by chance they needed a gamekeeper to shoot a deer at Greenwich, they would send a squad car to take us up there, but the gun had to be already at the park.

The week before the event took place we had a delivery at Richmond of 18km of crowd barriers, which had to be put up in the park from Roehampton Gate to Kingston Gate on both sides of the road, with gaps for the time being to allow deer to walk to and fro around the park.

The men's race was on Saturday, 28 July, and for Tony and me it was a 3 a.m. start. We met at Sheen Gate, and our job was to get as many of the deer to the centre of the park as possible. So any deer on the gate side of the road from Sheen to Kingston had to cross the road and be on the Pen Ponds side of the road. This meant that most of the park would be free for the deer to roam. Straight away we had problems: there were deer in large numbers all on the wrong side of the road from Kingston to Sheen. Wild deer don't take to being handled at all and if you want to move them you cannot herd them like cattle or sheep – they just won't do it. If you want them to go left they'll go right, or vice versa, so getting the animals to go through the gaps in the barriers was an excruciatingly slow task. You had to let them go through at their own pace because, if you tried to rush it, you would panic them and they would run anywhere.

Given time, they went through and, as they did so, we closed off all the gaps so they couldn't come back through again. We had to be finished before 6 a.m., which was when it was classified as lockdown and no one was allowed on the cycle route, so time was of the essence. There were a couple of times when deer jumped the barriers and they were knocking down a hundred metres of barrier at a time, running up and down the road trying to find a way off it. Thankfully, they did manage to escape and everything was in place waiting for the first riders to come through.

Tony and I also had to have our guns with us all day because if a deer were to jump the fence at the moment when all the cyclists were coming through and it had to be shot because of its injuries we wouldn't be able to get to our houses and get a gun. We were each given a zone to cover throughout the day. Mine was from Kingston Gate to White Ash Lodge drive, which could be covered only by going across country. A radio message came through to say the cyclists were due any second. I was covering an area that was to be the worst hot spot, at Ham Cross, and in front of me were a small group of fallow does looking desperately for a way across the road. They charged the barriers a couple of times, but thankfully didn't jump; then, just when I thought it was all going belly up, the cyclists turned up in a large group and it put them off.

Those damn does kept showing up throughout the day, but, thankfully, they didn't try their luck again. We had to stay on site until we were told to stand down, which didn't happen until 4 p.m. that day, so for me it was a thirteen-hour day and I don't mind admitting that I was knackered. Some staff did eighteen hours and some had to stay and sleep on the office floor because they wouldn't have been able to get into work the next day as the whole route for cycling was shut to all traffic. So it ended up being a very long weekend for all the park staff.

The next day we had to do it all again as it was the women's race, so it was another 3 a.m. start and all the same problems as the day before. Thankfully, nothing major happened, but I think we were very lucky. We had animals that were charging the barriers but didn't manage to cross the road. Had one done so right at the last minute you can imagine the uproar it would have caused and the injuries to riders doing fifty miles an hour, never mind the fact that a beautiful deer may well have had to be shot.

Just when we thought it was all over, Boris Johnson, who was Mayor of London at that time, decided he wanted to introduce something called RideLondon, which would take the exact same route as the Olympic cyclists took – straight through Richmond Park. You had to wonder if anyone had told those people that it was a deer park. Anyway, the following year it duly happened and continues to happen to this day. The amazing thing is there has never been an incident of a deer crashing into the cyclists, which is due to our efforts to get as many deer as possible into the right place before the race starts. I think that if a stag had charged the cyclists and caused a serious incident during the Olympic race, the suits might well have been put off holding RideLondon altogether.

In 2016 we had our worst year for deer jumping the barriers. They did it all the way from Sheen to Kingston and made our lives murder. It really is all hands to the pumps when it happens. I feel sorry for the deer because this is their home and we are the invaders. They obviously have their routes and ways of going through the day and then we come along and block everything off, so it throws them out of their comfort zone. I think we've been very fortunate so far. I hope I'm wrong, but it's odds on a disaster will happen one day.

Sadly, there is another aspect of these events that threatens the welfare of the deer and that is litter that is disposed of thoughtlessly by cyclists and those involved in similar activities such as duathlons. After the London Duathlon in September 2016, the Friends of Richmond Park, a charity dedicated to the conservation and protection of Richmond Park, conducted a review of the park on the Monday immediately after contracted litter pickers had swept the course route.

Along the grass verges of a 600m section from Pembroke Lodge to Richmond Gate, Friends volunteers found 161 empty gel packs and tear-off opening strips used by competing cyclists, as well as other litter. The Friends had carefully cleaned this section prior to the event. The full cycling course around Richmond Park (the main perimeter road) is nearly eleven kilometres so, although we cannot verify this, an extrapolation of the amount of litter found in the 600m survey would suggest there were many more litter items left around the park following the duathlon events, even though the event organisers had installed clear signs around the course stating, 'DON'T HARM THE DEER WITH LITTER! TAKE IT AWAY WITH YOU.'

Despite this and the provision of numerous bins and clear instructions on disposal of bottles and other race-related litter, it seems that many competitors ignored all of it and simply dropped litter without any thought in this environmentally sensitive area. The RideLondon event, which took place in the park in July, saw similar results with 182 gel packs and opening strips found in the same section. After both events, cleaning contractors used by the organisers to clear up failed to find these items.

These gel packs, and particularly the tear-off opening strips, are dangerous for deer as they are small enough to get hidden or trampled into the grass and undergrowth and mistakenly eaten by the animals. Litter can gradually clog the deer's digestive systems, leading to their being unable to eat properly and so eventually starving. Examinations of deer that have died unexpectedly often show their stomachs to be full of litter. Every year several of our herd die due to litter ingestion. When will people learn?

CHAPTER EIGHT

Moonlighting in Motion Pictures

As a complete contrast to the trials and tribulations of preserving an area of urban parkland from the unwittingly damaging attentions of millions of eager visitors, I'm often called on to be an unexpected film star, working with presenters from the BBC and film and television companies from all around the world, providing insight into just about every aspect of the park and its inhabitants. I've worked alongside all the top wildlife presenters, people such as Chris Packham, Nick Baker, Kate Humble, Bill Oddie, John Craven, and the doyen of them all, Sir David Attenborough.

A lot of these TV companies always seem to want the impossible, such as the time I was asked if they could see a deer being born. I said, 'I've seen it six times in thirty years, so good luck with that.' On another occasion I was asked if they could watch me ear-tagging young deer. I said, 'Last year me and my mate spent six weeks looking for new-borns to tag and we found just two. How long have you got?' When they said two days, I said, 'It might not happen.' Then, blow me! Talk about making you look a liar! I went out in the Flying Field – a wide open area of the park – and walked straight up to a young deer. I thought, I don't believe this. You little so and so. Why don't you just run away to prove my point? Anyway, I tagged him and the next day we found another one.

Once a company came in and wanted to do a piece on me and my job – which they did over the period of a week. I thought it was going to be all about the park and deer. They took lots of pictures and asked a thousand questions. No one was filming, just taking photos and recording and writing things down. A couple of months passed and suddenly a big, expensive, glossy magazine turned up in the post at the office featuring an article about the ten most wanted jobs in London. Mine came seventh. Not bad for a local lad who was always last in class at school and came out with no qualifications whatsoever. According to the magazine, I had a job that everyone wanted.

I also had an interesting experience with the BBC's Clare Balding, who came to the park to do a radio interview with me. We were walking across the Flying Field talking about the deer, and the subject turned to the infamous story of Fenton the dog, who became an Internet sensation in 2011. The incident had happened at almost the exact spot where Clare and I were walking; Fenton, a black Labrador, got away from his owner and began chasing after a herd of deer. Fenton ignored all the frantic shouting from his owner, who became increasingly desperate as his dog drove the frightened deer across the field and over the main through-road in the park. It was a miracle that they missed the steady streams of cars that were on the road at the time, which were forced to stop abruptly as the herd stampeded past.

The YouTube video, which was recorded by a thirteen-year-old boy on his iPhone, went viral with several million views. Most people found the episode hilarious, but I told Clare that I didn't think many of them appreciated just how dangerous that situation was. When deer are running flat out they can do thirty miles an hour, and it was sheer luck that the motorists saw them coming and were able to brake in time. But there was another side to it, which again was down to luck and could potentially have been disastrous. Imagine if a mother had been walking her baby in a pram across one of the footpaths or a family had been out for a walk. There could have been carnage, because once the deer are going flat out they won't stop for anything and they won't run round you, they'll just go charging on right over you.

When we'd finished the interview, Clare said to me, 'You've got an amazing deep voice – you could be the new Ray Winstone. You ought to do voiceovers.' I replied, 'Well, if you want someone to do Frankenstein's monster, I'm your man!' To tell the truth I wasn't on the show for long and I didn't even listen to it because I wasn't sure what radio frequency it was on.

I once worked with a Belgian film company and none of them spoke English very well. The guy who was interviewing me spoke what you might call pidgin English and, after struggling through the questions for my scene, he told me that he was going to repeat the scene but with questions in Belgian this time. I had to just nod and pretend I understood what he was talking about when I hadn't got a clue. He could have been calling me a nutcase for all I knew. On another occasion, I had to give a talk to thirty-odd Polish deer farmers, who also spoke virtually no English. The interpreter's English wasn't exactly brilliant either, so that was an interesting experience, to say the least.

As I mentioned earlier, the rut is a huge draw for film and television crews from across the globe. We've had the BBC down here countless times and I've worked with just about all of the top presenters, which has left me with a host of memories, many of them quite amusing. For example, a well-known presenter, who will remain nameless for obvious reasons, was filming a close-up of a stag for a nature programme and was becoming more and more nervous as the animal eyeballed him. Eventually, he said to me, 'What shall I do if he charges?' and I replied, 'Run like the flaming clappers!'

Once, I was doing a programme called *Countrywise* with Paul Heiney and we were in the Land Rover. I was driving, Paul was sitting beside me, there were the sound man and the producer in with us and the cameraman was in the back. The producer was talking to Paul, telling him not to forget to ask this and that. We were driving along and she said, 'Yes, I quite like that shot,' but the cameraman said, 'We can't have that because his hat's covering his face and making it look dark.' But she said, 'No, leave the hat on.' I thought they'd stopped filming when Paul said something to me about the rut. I replied, 'Well, at this time of year, mate, all it is, really, is sleeping, fighting and bonking, not necessarily in that order.' And he smiled.

When it came to watching the actual programme on TV, don't ask me how they did it, but they cut out all the stuff the producer said and the dialogue between Paul and me. You just heard me saying, 'It's all sleeping, fighting and bonking.' Well, of course, my colleagues gave me a right ribbing, saying, 'Trust Bartram to go on the telly and talk about sleeping, fighting and bonking.' That's all they remembered about the programme; they forgot about the rest!

On another occasion, I worked with a crew who wanted to film over a two-year period, covering things such as a deer being born and one being tagged. I was on it for twenty-five minutes, and it was all about me doing the job and the fact that it's in London. This particular programme picked certain people out around the London area. Another one was a guy who worked at Billingsgate fish market and was feeding a seal on the Thames every day. And one was an artist who photographed feral pigeons and she'd sit there with thousands of pigeons all over her.

As we have seen, these TV people always want the impossible, such as shots of young deer being born or being tagged, and of course these things don't just happen to order. I've had crews arriving in January and asking if they can film a deer being born and I've said, 'Well, good luck with that. They don't get born until June.' Or they'll arrive in February and say, 'We want to film them rutting.' And I'll say, 'Well, you're too late for that – that was in October, four months ago.' They're supposed to be the wildlife unit, but a lot of them haven't got a clue. They turn up here and come up with things they expect to film, and I have to tell them, 'That isn't going to happen.'

During the rut, the ace card for them is to film two stags fighting. I've gone out the day before filming, late evening time, and seen four stags with their stands on the Flying Field all really going for it. Then I've arrived there at seven the next morning with the film crew and there hasn't been a deer in sight for miles. So we've driven round and round for two hours and we haven't seen any deer at all, let alone stags giving it some welly with their antlers. I'm feeling a right plonker because I'm the head keeper and I can't even *find* the damn things, never mind film them. Never work with children or animals in showbiz they say – and I'll certainly second that.

I do enjoy it, though. It's great fun working with people such as John Craven, Paul Heiney, Chris Packham and Kate Humble. In that one-hour programme I did with Paul,

I had a twenty-minute feature slot, so I was a star myself for a little while. But it doesn't catapult you into fame; people didn't come up to me in the street and ask for my autograph! When I was working with Kate, who's a real star, she came over and was introducing herself when all of a sudden six bucks shot out into the middle of the road with a dog up their backsides chasing after them. Well, Kate didn't mess about: she was very assertive, telling the dog owner, 'Get your dog on a lead and under control.' I suppose that, being a farmer, she's used to dealing with that kind of scenario.

Kate was lovely to work with. We started about 9.30 a.m. and we filmed for almost three hours. They asked me loads of quick-fire questions about this and that, but in the end I was on TV for just a few seconds. I remember the stags were fighting and one of them got up and piddled down his belly, and I told Kate that he was scenting. And she smiled and said, 'Yes, I can see he's scenting all right.'

Apart from working with many of the leading lights (and perhaps a few of the lesser lights!) of television, I have come across numerous TV and film stars in Richmond Park. The area is a highly desirable place to live, and so it attracts people from that world. The actor Sir John Mills used to live just outside the gates at Richmond and I used to see him quite often. He lived in a house called The Wick on the corner of Nightingale Road, which is on top of Richmond Hill, a stone's throw from Richmond Gate. It is said that the sound of the wind whistling around the house inspired Mills's wife, the actress and writer Mary Hayley Bell, to write the novel *Whistle Down the Wind*, which was made into a film and musical by Andrew Lloyd Webber. Sir John sold the house but a few years later came back and bought it again as he liked it so much. Today the house is owned by Pete Townshend, of rock group The Who, who bought it from Ronnie Wood, guitarist for the Rolling Stones, who purchased it from Mills.

My father sometimes had to do guard duty outside The Wick after it was taken over by the military as a base during World War Two. The park and the immediate area around it was the centre for various military activities during the war. David Niven, the Hollywood star, was one of the officers for the GHQ Liaison Regiment, known as Phantom, which was based in Pembroke Lodge in the park, and trained armoured-car personnel and motorcycle riders equipped with radios to patrol the battlefront in Europe and relay intelligence to the commanders of Allied units.

Jerry Hall came in once a few years back to open the Tamsin Trail cycle path round the park, and I have often seen Ronnie Wood, who lived on nearby Kingston Hill, driving through in his green, open-topped Bentley. Down the bottom of Star and Garter Hill you will find the home of actor Richard E. Grant, who is often in here riding his horse. Next door to the park on Petersham Road is Montrose House, a seventeenth-century Grade II listed building, where singer and actor Tommy Steele used to live.

Just a short walk from The Wick you will find the home of the most celebrated of all wildlife broadcasters, Sir David Attenborough, who frequently comes into Richmond Park to assist with filming and charity work. Sir David's late brother, Richard, the actor, director and producer, used to live on the corner of Richmond Green. It is quite common to see some of today's stars in and around the park.

In June 2016 Sir David Attenborough came here to play his part in an educational film being made by the Friends of Richmond Park. This was the first time I'd been directly involved with the biggest name of them all. Sir David lives little more than a stone's throw from the park and in the foreword to the Friends' book, *Guide to Richmond Park*, he revealed what the park means to him by saying:

Richmond Park is a very special place for me. My regular walks in the park (sadly very restricted nowadays), with its peace and tranquillity, have always provided me with an invaluable respite from the strains of everyday life.

The Park's wildlife is exceptional, particularly for somewhere so close to a major urban centre. It well deserves its designation as a Site of Special Scientific Interest and a National Nature Reserve (given, incidentally, for its veteran trees, acid grassland and stag beetles – aspects of the Park we tend to overlook in our enthusiasm for the views and the deer).

The film is designed to be an educational and training tool for the public and schools. They wanted me to do something about litter and the effect it has on deer, but they ran out of time and it was postponed to later in the year. When I got this job I never thought I'd be working with all the wildlife stars, and now I've ended my career with the biggest of the lot, a man who's more than just a famous wildlife presenter: he's a household name and a national treasure.

It was the first time I'd met Sir David, although I'd sometimes seen him around Richmond, and, to be honest, I was a little in awe of him. My sister-in-law had been lucky enough to meet him at her workplace, Butterfly World in Hertfordshire, of which he was a great supporter until it had to close. So, when I was asked to go and pick him up from his house and bring him to the park for the filming, Ron Crompton, chairman of the Friends of Richmond Park, came with me and knocked on Sir David's door while I waited in the car, a little anxiously.

Well, Sir David came out and got in the front beside me. He was all smiles and said, 'Hello, how are you?' and I said, 'Belated happy birthday!' And that broke the ice. I said to him, 'How are you doing?' and he replied, 'Sometimes I feel ninety and sometimes I don't.'

Then I said, 'You've had bad knees, haven't you? Have you had them done?' and he replied 'Yes, it's brilliant. It's taken twenty years off me.' So I said, 'You're not doing so bad, but you're not doing as well as my mum. She's ninety-three.'

Anyway, he came into the park and did his scene, which, incidentally, he did without charging a fee because the Friends are a charity and the film will help educate people about the park and its ecology. He was talking about the veteran oak trees round by Sidmouth Wood and, after he had delivered his lines in his inimitable way, I had to whisk him back home again. I remember my sister-in-law saying that he was such an interesting man and interested in everything you say, which was exactly my impression of him, too. He is a true professional and likes everything to be in place when he arrives, which is only to be expected when he's in such demand and his time is so valuable. This particular window of time was the only one he had available in his hectic schedule.

The cameraman was someone he's worked with for about forty years, whom they managed to get hold of for that slot. The director had worked with Sir David as well, so everything went smoothly. As I've learned many times with these filming jobs, there's usually lots of hanging around for just a few minutes of actual filming. I can totally understand why Sir David wants to turn up and have everything ready so he can get the job done and be on to the next one. When he arrives, he walks straight out in front of the camera and says what's needed. It's not scripted; it's all off the top of his head because he's done so much in that whole area that he knows exactly what to say and when to say it.

During the course of the day, I was driving him from Sidmouth Wood to Isabella Plantation and I asked him if he'd always lived in the area. He said that he hadn't but that when his daughters were younger he used to come into the park a lot, but he doesn't come in so much nowadays. I mentioned his late brother Richard, the actor and director, who also used to live in Richmond, and, although he understandably didn't say much about that, he was very chatty. He asked about various aspects of my job and was interested in everything I did.

At one point he amazed me by saying, 'I hear you're leaving,' and when I said yes he said, 'Why? What are you leaving for?' When I told him I was retiring, the indefatigable ninety-year-old exclaimed, 'Retire? You can't retire. You're not old enough!' I replied, 'Well, there's an old saying: "Make hay while the sun shines."'

You might sum up Sir David by saying that he's an ambassador for wildlife and one thing he makes very clear is something he has in common with Chris Packham: the belief that there are too many of us on this planet. There simply aren't enough resources for all of us. Something needs to be done if we want this planet to survive. The problem is that people live only for the day. They can't see past the ends of their noses.

CHAPTER NINE

All Creatures Small and Pesky

We call Richmond Park wild and, by modern standards, it is. But there is little real wild nature left in Britain, and human activity has results that need redressing. As the gamekeeper, I had a duty to cull any species that destroyed habitats and flora and fauna, or posed a danger to the human users of the Park.

At times I'm an office clerk, tied to my desk and writing reports, planning deer management and the deer culls in November and February. But I'm also a pest controller, targeting squirrels, rabbits, feral pigeons and other birds such as crows, magpies and jackdaws, who pull rubbish out of the bins, which is then eaten by the deer, for whom it can be harmful and even fatal. In fact we keep an eye on a wide range of creatures, and you'll be amazed what we find. We carry out pest control all year round, but when there's more daylight we tend to shoot the animals. Keepers on conventional rural estates would throw up their hands at what we have to do, and at the constraints on how we do it. When I started, the Park was less visited, and it was possible to use our guns throughout the day. Nowadays we have to squeeze our daylight shooting into the hours when the public is not there – early morning and late evening – all, of course, in the summer months.

For instance, most days, in July, we'll be out early in the mornings doing pest control. When I first came we had pheasant and partridges to tend to, so we'd do our pest control and then we'd look after our birds. We did things like 'bitting', which involved plastic rings going over their beaks to stop them pulling out their feathers, which we had to do, otherwise we'd end up with hundreds of bald birds. They'd get bored and pluck at one another, so you had to keep their minds active. I'd do things such as hanging a lettuce upside down because they love lettuce, and sometimes I'd get a wet lettuce and put it in an ants' nest, so it was covered in ants – anything to keep the boredom away.

In days gone by, we'd work from six in the morning until noon and then from seven to nine in the evening. They had rabbits on the golf course in plague proportions. There were thousands of them. Dave Smith and I would go up there at night and he'd be shooting one side, and I the other, so we wouldn't accidentally shoot one another. There were so many of them that we never seemed to be getting anywhere. We ferreted there one day and we had a hundred and ninety rabbits out of one warren and then we came back the following morning after we'd filled in all the holes and we had a further eighty.

We are very restricted in what we can do. We can't gas rabbits because we've got badgers and foxes. You can legally gas foxes, but the park has around 5.5 million visitors each year and I reckon about 3 million of them come into the park with dogs. You can't guarantee that Mrs Jones's dog isn't going to dig a hole where you've just gassed rabbits and end up killing itself.

I did use wax-coated gas pellets at Kew when I worked there. These are placed down the rabbit hole with the use of a long tube. Then you put turf upside down over the hole and backfill it with soil, so that when the pellets hit the moist soil inside, the gas is released and it flows upwards and forms a pocket near the top of the hole. People sometimes ask why we need to kill cute little bunnies – as they see them – and there's a simple answer: they are pests. They create problems by digging holes on the greens of the golf course; they eat bedding plants – which cost thousands of pounds – in places such as Pembroke Lodge; and they strip bark off trees up to eighteen inches off the ground, working their way around the whole tree so it eventually dies. It's not about eradication; it's about keeping the numbers under control. You wouldn't be able to get rid of them all, anyway. You're trying to create vacuums. So, for example, we tried to create a vacuum in Isabella Plantation long enough for the plants to establish themselves and to thrive.

There are times when I see all sorts of coloured rabbits in the park, from black and white to all grey. These are pets that people have let go because they are too big to look after any longer. These animals have a chance of surviving because we have a high population of rabbits in the park and they have all the food they need. However, William Cathcart, a former assistant superintendent, was on holiday once, and someone went into his garden and put a rabbit in the hutch alongside his rabbit. When he came home he spotted it straight away and, to make matters worse, it was a buck that had been put in with a doe, so he ended up with lots of baby rabbits.

I had the same thing happen but in a different way. I came down to go to work one morning and found an empty box outside my front door. I thought nothing more of it until I came home a little later, just as the dustmen were taking the bins, and one of them said to me 'Have you seen the rabbit in your front garden?' I said, 'Rabbit – what rabbit?' and he said, 'Over there.' Sure enough, there was this great big, fat rabbit just lying there. My wife Maggie came out, picked it up and put it in a cage and it bit her. We ended up keeping this unwanted pet and it would try to bite you every time you went into its pen. When it eventually died, it was a relief, to be honest. The sheer cheek some people have just dumping animals like this on others and expecting them to take care of them defies belief.

Shooting squirrels in trees is not very profitable in summer – you can't see enough of them. The best time to shoot squirrels is in March, by 'poking' their dreys. Unfortunately this is a lively and highly visible activity, and would not go down well with the public. When the leaves comes off the trees, it's already getting dark by 4 p.m., and anyway they are starting to hibernate. So not a lot can be done in the short daylight hours. That's the reason we set traps. We use Kania traps, which are mounted on trees about eight feet above the ground, where they don't pose a danger to the public. We also pick places where the public aren't allowed, but that doesn't mean to say that they won't go to those places and interfere with them. If they're stupid enough to put their fingers in a trap, they won't be tapping away at their computer keyboard or playing piano next day; their fingers would be chopped in half. The traps kill the squirrels humanely, and we have about thirty of them placed around the park. They need to be checked every twenty-four hours, although if we're catching quite a few, we'll do it twice a day.

I have often found ferrets running round the park, some of which I have kept because they have been quite friendly. Others I've done away with, because all they wanted to do was bite. This happens when people have come in poaching rabbits and the ferret has stayed down the hole and come up much later after they've gone. This sort of animal can survive quite easily as there are plenty of rabbits to feed on. Like mink, they are very versatile and can climb trees and eat eggs and chicks just like mink. From an ecological point of view, they are a disaster and need to be taken out as soon as seen.

Our early start is necessary in order to get pest control out of the way with guns before the public start to emerge. We continue with pest control right through to September, which sounds a long time but, for control work, is relatively short. As I said, most estate keepers have all year, but we have to get it done while we can.

In the case of Richmond Park, pest control is not always confined to the usual species. I remember once I got a team together to net Ham Pond, to try to eradicate the terrapins that were in there in large numbers and doing a lot of damage to other wildlife. These creatures arrived in the park because the public had bought them as pets and then no longer wanted to keep them when they got too big. So, rather than do something else with them, they released them into the park thinking they were doing a good thing, whereas in reality they were not. One of our blokes named Alex Patterson was helping and was wearing chest waders, which are like a big pair of trousers up to the armpits. We hadn't been going five minutes when he fell over and what seemed like two thousand gallons of pond water rushed into his waders. You've never seen anything so funny. He looked like Billy Bunter and was having trouble walking, and with such a weight of water in his waders he couldn't even stand properly. What was more interesting was that he had fish in there with him. I complained that he didn't catch a terrapin.

Foxes are very common in suburban London. They can easily come in and out of the Park, and do so. There's an old saying that, when you see your first bluebell, it's time to see young foxes and badger cubs being born, as well as deer. Once, back in 1995, I was out on my own with my gun doing pest control as my mate was on leave. Around 6.30 a.m., a guy flagged me down to tell me that there was a puppy on its own right in the middle of the Flying Field at Sheen. When I got there I discovered it was a fox cub, which had just opened its eyes and couldn't have been more than three or four weeks old. I picked it up and put it in the footwell on the passenger side of the Land Rover.

I'm sure that most of you will at some point have done something that seems like a good idea at the time, but that you later come to regret. This was one of those moments. I decided to take the little fellow home and show him to my wife Maggie, as she would never have seen a fox cub, let alone have handled one. I told her to come into the garden, close her eyes and hold out her hands. She asked me if it was wet or sticky and I told her, 'No, just sit down, close your eyes and hold out your hands.' I was already wondering if I was doing the right thing and, when I dropped it into her hands and she opened her eyes, she started crying her eyes out because she knew I was going to do away with him. She then proceeded to call me every name under the sun and tell me how cruel I was, and it was then I knew for sure that I had made a major boob.

The next thing I knew I was down at the vet's getting puppy milk and a syringe to feed this cub, which we named Lucky, because he was lucky to be alive. Over the next week Lucky proceeded to chew every boot, chair leg, and table leg in our house and pee all over the joint. After that he was kept in an old tack room in the works yard. When he reached sixteen weeks, he was too big to keep indoors, so I made a home for him in an old pheasant release pen and kept him in there where no one would come into contact with him. I finally opened the door and he went on his way, and I hope he had a good life. I know for sure that, if I'd left him in the Flying Field, the first dog to come along would have killed him. Anyway, it was a lovely experience for both of us.

I remember receiving a call from a park resident concerning 'unwanted guests' in one of the park lodges. He said to me, 'Could you come up to the house, please. I think we've got mice.' Talk about an understatement! When I got there and went into the kitchen I'd never seen anything like it. There were mouse droppings everywhere – all over the worktops, every pot, pan, plate and bowl – everything you could see had a dropping in it. When we sat down and had a cup of tea, I was thinking, I hope this mug hasn't got mouse droppings in it.

I said to him, 'You've got to be really careful because they'll have been piddling everywhere, so there's a serious danger of Weil's disease or leptospirosis – you could end up killing yourselves.' I said that everything had to be washed before it was used. Then I came back up again with a dozen boxes of poison and we put them all round the house. I said I'd return in a couple of weeks, but told him that he should check the boxes because they might need refilling. When I did go back, he said that the problem seemed to be sorted because they'd had no more droppings.

When you live in the park, it's difficult to stop mice coming into your house, along with huge spiders – it goes with the territory. Wood mice in particular come in during the winter months. If they can find a way in, they will; they can get through the tiniest cracks and holes.

Much of our pest control concerns creatures even smaller than mice – the abundant insect life of the Park. One night I was woken at 2 a.m. by wasp stings to my chest and arm. My wife Maggie helped me to kill the wasp and we didn't think any more of it. A couple of weeks passed and we received a callout for a wasp nest on the golf course, so later that evening I went up there with Dave, the head keeper, to deal with it. While I was spraying the nest, one stung me on the back of my hand and almost immediately I started to feel faint and I blacked out. After twenty minutes I came round with Dave standing over me asking if I was all right. At this point I felt OK, got up and looked in the wing mirror to see a face covered in mud. I asked Dave what had happened and he said, 'Well, I didn't know what to do, so I put my hankie in that muddy puddle and dabbed it on your face to try to bring you round.' I said, 'I look like I've been down a coal mine.'

At this point I didn't have a clue what was going on in the bigger picture, so another couple of weeks passed and I was picking elderberries in my back garden for Maggie when a wasp stung me on the head. I sat down and rolled a cigarette, and suddenly my ears started to really itch.

Maggie was beginning to panic, but I told her I felt fine. Then, as I went to stand up, I felt really faint. Maggie and my brother Dave took me to hospital and they rushed me through to a cubicle in A&E, where a nurse was taking my blood pressure every minute. Apparently I didn't have any blood pressure!

I remember looking at my hand and seeing huge red welts forming and linking up. Then I felt my eyes closing and my mouth and tongue swelling, and I was having difficulty breathing. The next thing I remember was waking up next to a huge monitor with nurses all around me and discovering that I'd been there overnight in intensive care.

The registrar gave me a letter and told me to see my GP immediately, which I did. The GP told me that if I was to be stung on the way to the chemist from the surgery, I could be a dead man because I'd had an anaphylactic reaction to wasp venom. He told me to come back the following day and said that he would show me how to inject myself with adrenaline.

To this day I have to carry an EpiPen, a device that delivers adrenaline shots as my life-saving drug. I did go to a unit in Brompton Hospital over a period of ten years to be desensitised, but eventually it was decided that continuing with treatment would not benefit me. When they did tests on me, it turned out that I was allergic to one-millionth of a wasp sting, and they said that I was extremely lucky to be alive with such a reaction. Ironically, I have never been stung since that year, but I often think about the potential danger lurking all around me from one of the tiniest creatures in the park.

Smaller still is a really serious pest, only recently arrived in the Park. One of our main tasks during May and June takes up so much time – around eight hours a day – that there's very little scope for anything else. If I tell you that the task involves looking up oak trees with binoculars, you might well wonder what on earth we're looking for and why. The 'what' is the oak processionary moth (OPM), its nests and caterpillars. When we find them we record data about the number of nests, the sites and other details. The 'why' is because those little critters can defoliate oaks as efficiently as locusts and their caterpillar hairs are toxic. If they come into contact with your skin, eyes or lungs you will need medical treatment, and obviously the deer would be affected by them as well. I trod on a fallen nest once and my ankle was like a balloon for two weeks and itched like crazy. I had sandals on and I thought it was a Jenny Wren's nest, so I rolled it with my foot. Mind you, I've been bitten by just about every bug and tick known to man during my time here – it's an occupational hazard.

Weeks on end looking up those trees really strains the neck muscles and towards the end I feel my neck is so wide that I look like Kermit the Frog. I'll go on holiday to Cornwall with Maggie and we'll be walking around a park or gardens somewhere and she'll say, 'For God's sake, stop looking up oak trees.' And I'll say, 'I can't help it.' It's monotonous and stressful but it has to be done. Once they've all been located and mapped, the whole of July is spent with specialist pest-removal gangs going round the park getting rid of them.

The saga begins around the end of May when Tony and I are given a zone in the park, a GPS unit, yellow tags, hammers, nails and marker pens. You're looking for clusters of caterpillars. They're quite easy to spot because they're at what experts call stage seven, which means they're quite big with large white hairs, which they're shedding all the time. You can't miss them because they're hanging down in great big globules underneath the branches. It looks pretty horrible, like something out of an *Alien* movie.

We count how many nests or clusters we see and we mark them down, together with the zone they're in, and the tree number. This year, one of our trees had more than a hundred nests in it and they were all the way along every one of the branches. We bring all that data back to the office and then the arboricultural officer logs it on the computer. Then she prints out a map of the park showing where all the yellow dots are, and when we look at the map it seems as if there are about forty million yellow dots on it. The arboricultural officer has around forty volunteers to help her because we've only got the month of June to get every tree counted and recorded.

Once the data has all been recorded and it gets to July, everything else stops. Tony and I are each allocated a gang, or maybe two gangs, and we go around the various zones. We're looking for the nests while the pest-control guys go up the trees in cherry pickers. I'll be saying to one guy, 'OK, you've got one to your right, and another to your left.' And he might say that he can't see the one on the right, but I've got a laser light, which I can point to help him. He'll collect as many nests as he can from the tree and bag them up. While they're collecting the caterpillars, the gang are suited and booted like spacemen. They have to wear protective suits, goggles and gloves, which shows you just how dangerous those hairy little creatures are. They throw the bags full of caterpillars into our incinerator and at the end of the day I incinerate the lot.

In Holland and Germany, where they've got commercial woodlands, OPMs have defoliated hundreds of acres of oak. The floor is so heavily laden with caterpillar hairs that it's a dangerous environment for people to walk around in and they've had to section off vast areas. What concerns me most from a professional point of view is that deer can't read 'KEEP OUT' signs. And what do deer love? Acorns. So they can be nosing around looking for acorns and they might come across a fallen nest of OPM caterpillars. It's a miracle it hasn't happened yet, but I've often thought it's only a matter of time before I come across a deer with its nose, tongue and mouth all blistered. I came across two huge nests in one summer that were so heavy with the weight of caterpillars in them that they'd fallen out of the tree. It was pure chance that we spotted them and we had to get the gang in to come and pick them up.

The females lay their eggs underneath tiny little

branches, near where the buds are. When the buds pop, the caterpillars emerge. In the first stage after they're born they're tiny and they're pink. It's the only time you can spray them effectively with pesticide, because their skin is penetrable. Once they get to stage two or three, their skin has hardened and it's very difficult to kill them then, because we only use a mild pesticide, not wanting to kill every insect off. Sometimes we spend ages spraying meticulously and then it rains heavily and the whole lot gets washed away. It's expensive, but it does work: we've seen quite a reduction in the number of nests where we've sprayed.

It's a devil of a job overall and I've known some years when it's taken up three and a half months, and I've had to say to the superintendent and the arboricultural officer, 'Look, this has got to stop. Technically, as a herdsman, I should be looking at my herd once every twenty-four hours. I haven't looked out there for six weeks – I don't even know if I've got any deer left. They could all be dead for all I know.' I told them that I needed to get out there, so we had to come to an arrangement, but it still takes up at least two months of the year.

The OPM problem has been in the park for about eight or nine years and, believe it or not, it came from Kew Gardens. It wasn't their fault. There was a private development behind Kew and the developers went to Holland to buy some oak trees because they were the cheapest. They brought them back to Kew not realising they had OPM eggs on them, which subsequently hatched.

As Kew Gardens is all about plants rather than wildlife, they sprayed their oaks with pesticide, but it didn't wipe them all out; even to this day you still get half a dozen trees there with the odd nest in them.

They've now extended out even further than Richmond Park. They've reached places such as Reading and Wisley Gardens, the Royal Horticultural Society site. Apparently, we're one of the few places doing their utmost to control it. When the OPMs first arrived, we thought we would be able to eradicate the problem, but then it was decided that the best we'd be able to do was to keep them within Richmond Park, so now it's a question of 'Can we manage it?' The idea now is that we'll hit hotspots, so we might go out and do all the restaurant and car park areas, places where people congregate in large numbers. And areas where we found a lot one year, such as Sheen Cross woods, are sprayed, so that, hopefully, there won't be as many in the following year.

It is also that time of year when acorns are appearing, which is why it is so important that we continue removing OPMs, even though it feels like we're flogging a dead horse because it's only a matter of time before a deer gets those caterpillar hairs in its eyes and mouth and has to be dispatched. This problem is not going away.

Each year in May and June we always have to call on our local beekeepers. It happens when we have a large swarm hanging from a branch, which is nearly always right over a footpath. It's fascinating to watch: the beekeeper gets the queen out of his pocket in a tiny cage and puts it into a box, and then he shakes the branch where the bees are all hanging to make them fall on the ground. Then they all start walking along the ground into this box and he shuts the door and takes them away. Weird, but wonderful. I did once get hold of a guy who specialised in moving hornets and he came and moved a nest for me. He put it deeper in the woods so they were still in the same area that they knew but out of harm's way. That takes balls, I can tell you. But he did it – with me watching at a great distance. It's like with wasps, we won't kill any animal or insect unless there's a good reason and no other option.

CHAPTER TEN

Buster and Snod

We don't usually get to know individual deer, or become attached to them, first because we understand that they are wild animals, but also because there are six hundred of them roaming freely around the park, which can make it difficult to recognise any one deer. But there was one notable exception to the rule, a quirk of nature so rare that I wouldn't have believed it if I hadn't been the one to experience it myself.

I must admit that I had a tear in my eye when I was forced to say goodbye to an old friend, a stag who was a real one-off. He first grabbed my attention back in the noughties, when I was doling out the winter feed from the back of our Land Rover. From November to April we give the deer special pellets and maize as a supplement to make sure they're getting their proper supply of vitamins and minerals. If they become deficient in selenium and copper they can suffer from what's known as 'sway back' or 'staggers', which makes them roll around as if they're drunk.

One night during the feed a young stag started walking towards me. He came closer and closer until he was right up against the back of the Land Rover. I couldn't believe it because, as we've seen, the deer in the park are truly wild animals and don't like getting too close to humans. But this one made it obvious he wanted personal attention. I noticed that he had bent brow tines (antler branches) – the ones nearest to his eyes. He had one sticking up and one pointing down, and his personality was just as characterful as his looks. He made a big impact on many people, not just me.

When he was right up close to the Land Rover, I held out some feed in my hand and to my amazement he took it right from me. He did the same thing the following night, and the night after that. He was a clumsy animal, and when feeding, he would lower his head but his antlers were so big that they would get in the way and often hit something. Eventually, he got into the habit of rattling his antlers against the back of the Land Rover when it was feeding time. He became so impatient one night that he rammed his antlers into the rear lights and smashed them to pieces. After that there was really only one name we could give him. From that day on, he was known as Buster, and he became part of the legend of the park.

As one element of the educational activities of Holly

Lodge, the park office, we give talks to local children about the deer and we take them out feeding at night. Learning from the Land Rover runs, Buster also got into the habit of coming up to the back door and rattling it loudly when it was coming up for feeding time. He would also press his face right up against the window and stare you out. The kids loved it, they screamed with delight, and dinnertime with Buster became the highlight of their evening.

And he was a bit of lad in other ways, too. On one occasion during the rutting season I received a call saying there was a dead stag on Broomfield Hill. When I got there I found Buster lying flat out, looking so still and lifeless that I felt sure he was dead. I took hold of his antlers and went to drag him away somewhere where he wouldn't be obvious to the public. However, as soon as I started he hauled himself to his feet and looked me in the eye as if to say, 'What the hell do you think you're doing?' He was just totally exhausted, having bonked himself silly with all the girls he could get hold of. I was called out several times in quick succession during the rut when he was supposed to be dead but turned out to be fast asleep.

When he was coming up to fourteen – a good age for a stag – I realised that I hadn't seen him for a while. The next time he crossed my path I was shocked to see that he'd suddenly deteriorated and was looking extremely sad and sorry for himself. He looked like a hundred-year-old man who's finding everything an effort and thinking, when's the end going to come? It's difficult to tell the age of deer just by looking at them, but they're a bit like humans: when they're young, they're upright and supple like swans; as they get older, gravity kicks in and everything starts to get flabbier and head south.

He'd picked up quite a few wounds over the years and he was a shadow of the magnificent animal he had been in his prime when he looked like the classic Highland stag in Sir Edwin Landseer's nineteenth-century painting *The Monarch of the Glen*. He'd taken to hiding away in a corner of the park where he knew he wouldn't be bothered. It broke my heart having to shoot him, because this was the only deer I grew attached to in my thirty years at the park. But in the end it was the kindest thing to do. In the normal course of events I'd have taken him out earlier, but I kept him on beyond his time because of who he was. I don't usually allow master stags more than two years at the top because you get groups of hinds who will frequent the same area, and stags are also creatures of habit, so they'll often go back to the same stands year after year. This means that you could get a stag mating with his own daughter and that's something we try to avoid at all costs.

Buster will always have a special place in my memory. I decided to honour him by getting his head and antlers mounted and placed on a wall in the office. There's a plaque underneath detailing his life story. Even though I'm moving on, Buster will remind everyone who passes through Holly Lodge of a special deer in the park's history. There's also what you might call a living memorial to him as well, because he was certainly a potent old devil and a good many of the young deer out there now are his progeny.

There was, in truth, one other animal that became very special to me during my thirty years in Richmond Park – my black Labrador, Snod. Dogs truly are extraordinary creatures. We have selectively bred them for thousands of years, and one of the reasons we have for doing so is simply for them to be our companions and, yes, our friends. And, as every keeper knows, in every lifetime, as with human friendships, there is always one special one.

When the month of showers and daffodils comes around I can't help thinking back to one particularly sad April day when I lost my best gun dog and best friend, Snod. The date was 18 April 2000, to be exact – it's ingrained on my memory. The reason I had a gun dog was to retrieve anything I shot while doing pest control. The aim was to stop anything running off wounded and bring it back for me to dispatch.

I named him Snod because a good friend of mine called Rodney Woods, who taught me everything I knew about pheasants and partridges, also had a Labrador called Snod. Rodney owned Pond Farm, near Wisley Gardens in Surrey, and the remarkable thing was that he never shouted at Snod. He talked to him like a human being:

'What do you think you're doing?' or 'Get back indoors' – that kind of thing. And Snod would always respond as if he understood perfectly.

I bought my Snod as a puppy in May 1989, at thirteen weeks old. There were only two left in the litter – he and a bitch. The bitch was very forward and came over to me straightaway, but Snod sat down at the end of the room and didn't want to know. This made me take to him immediately. I liked the fact that he didn't want to jump all over me like the bitch and piddle everywhere.

I had him eleven years; he went wherever I went and was always beside me. In all of that period he barked only three times – I've never known such a quiet dog. He never whimpered or made a sound, and I sometimes had to look to see if he was next to me because of his quietness. It was so long before he did bark that I began to wonder if there was something wrong with. But when he was just over a year old, we heard him growling and barking and going bonkers. I wondered what on earth he was up to and thought, whatever it is he's growling at, he's going to rip it to pieces. When we got outside, we saw it was a sun beetle climbing the wall. I assumed that it was the first time he'd ever seen one. But, at this point, I started to wonder if I'd bought a lunatic.

I began his training very early and he was just a delight to be with. Some lessons I showed him only once and he never forgot them to the day he died. He was so intelligent and easy to train that in no time at all I had him sitting and retrieving and watching for his next command. Eventually,

I felt sure that he could read my mind, because sometimes he would do what I wanted him to do without my having to say anything. He turned out to be an amazing dog and just a lovely animal, totally devoted to Mags and me.

He did have some dirty habits, though. He was always slobbering huge globules of saliva all over me whenever I put on a clean pair of trousers. But his strangest characteristic was that he ate almost literally everything, from wood to frozen horse manure; anything he could swallow, he would. I remember one Boxing Day when he kept running up to me every five minutes with a whole cooked turkey in his mouth. These were turkeys that people had thrown over the park wall assuming foxes would eat them.

As time went on he would get very excited in the morning when he saw the gun because he knew what it meant and he enjoyed the work so much. It was a job to keep him quiet at 5.30 a.m. and I lived in fear of waking the neighbours. There were times when he frightened the life out of me, especially when he would jump head first into a great big chunk of bramble with 'man-eating' thorns to retrieve what I'd shot. But he would come out two minutes later with a squirrel, thorns sticking out of his head and a big smile – the loony!

Then there were times when he really excelled. For example, I remember coming down to Pen Ponds and a guy had thrown a retrieve dummy – a small canvas bag filled with lightweight material that simulates shot game – into the pond so far out that his puppy was exhausted and couldn't find it. I called Snod to heel, sat him down and threw a small stick to where the dummy was and sent him in. He went straight to the dummy and brought it back to me. This bloke was gobsmacked and couldn't praise him and me enough. I felt like king of the castle for a moment. Another time, when I was ill and Mags walked him, he was off at a distance when two horse riders came cantering through; she just put her hand up and he sat straight down right next to the horse track and stayed until the horses had gone. She was so proud of him.

I couldn't have asked for a better dog. He was everything in one. Sadly, his habit of eating everything was to be his undoing. On 10 April he became ill and kept vomiting. I took him to the vets and they did numerous tests but, while we were waiting for these to come back, on the morning of the 18th he couldn't get up and was lying in his own mess. I knew instantly that the time had come to say goodbye. And, of all the things I've done in my life, this was to be the hardest. I called the vet and he arrived within minutes. What we didn't know was that he had eaten a whole pigeon days before that had the botulism virus and it was this that had caused the paralysis, for which there was no cure. I stayed with Snod to the end and we buried him in the back garden where he had grown up and loved to be. Maggie and I shed a few tears that day.

When I first arrived here Dave Smith, the head keeper, had a Jack Russell called Charlie. We went out shooting one morning and, while I was getting my gun and bag out, Charlie was barking like mad chasing a squirrel. When I turned round Charlie was twenty feet up a tree chasing the squirrel, jumping from branch to branch like a monkey, with this squirrel up above him hanging from the highest limbs. I'd never seen anything like it before and I thought I was hallucinating. How he climbed the tree I don't know, but he was totally at ease jumping from branch to branch, and he did this often on other trees.

I also had a terrier called Toby and, on the same day as Charlie's tree exploit, we were parked on Killcat Bridge over Beverley Brook and opened the back door to let the dogs out. Toby jumped right out of the Land Rover and right off the bridge, a fall of at least twenty feet. He landed in the brook and, luckily, there was about a foot of water to break his fall. Following that incident, he wouldn't walk through puddles or any water again. He would rather walk twenty miles round it because that experience had frightened him off for good.

Most estate keepers have at least two or three dogs for various uses. At Richmond I haven't needed a full kennel. But I became all the more fond of that single, special dog.

CHAPTER ELEVEN

Royals and Royal Parks

R ichmond is one of eight Royal Parks in London. Of these, only Bushy Park and Greenwich also have herds of deer. They are run by the government – although that is about to change – which makes my job very different from that of an estate keeper in the countryside.

When I started I never imagined that I would be serving venison from the park to the Queen and other members of her family, including Prince Charles, the Queen Mother, the Duke of Edinburgh and Princess Margaret, nor did I realise that I would be serving her government with a free haunch, which was provided under a warrant by the Queen. At the time Margaret Thatcher was prime minister, and all the Members of Parliament in her government qualified for this perk, as did some members of the House of Lords. I went on to serve the next prime minister, John Major, and dignitaries such as the Grand Falconer of England and the Master of the Horse. In fact, I was pitched straight into serving the Royal Warrant just two days after I started, when I was straight into my first cull. It did feel a bit weird to be holding a leg of venison that the Queen or the Prime Minister would be eating.

In 1986, when I arrived, there were seven hundred staff directly employed by the Royal Parks. Now it's a hundred and ten (up from around thirty-five in 1993). Redundancies have taken their toll of directly employed staff. But the total number of people managing and operating the parks is still probably more than seven hundred, if contractors' and concessionaires' staff are included.

I was fortunate because, although Dave and I were on the list of people to be made redundant, we were saved at the very last moment. In fact, I've been on a redundancy list twice in my years of working here and both times escaped it, so I've been a lucky man. But times are changing again: the Royal Parks will no longer be run by the government because it is going to become a charitable trust. Exactly how this will change things no one knows at the time of writing, but big changes are inevitable, although they obviously won't affect me.

What a lot of people don't realise is that up to now, as a result of the Royal Parks' constitution, anything major that we wanted to do had to be passed through Parliament as an Act. So, for example, the reduction of the speed limit to twenty miles an hour and the shutting of Robin Hood Gate both had to be put through

Parliament and then become law. Any time you see a sign that says, 'By order of the Secretary of State', you know it's been passed into law. I think that has been a good thing because we couldn't just do as we pleased. The downside is that any change could take ages, because if the minister misses the cut-off point in Parliament, it goes to the back of the queue. Although we have regulations in the park, they would have had to go through Parliament, including all laws about dogs and poaching and wildlife crime in general.

With all the Royal Parks under one administration, it was natural that the deer expertise and other keeping experience of the Richmond team should be shared out among the other parks. We had regular duties to perform in the other parks, and frequently had to help out on an ad hoc basis. One job we would do every three years was to dart a stag and a buck and take them up to Greenwich Park, whose cull we have always carried out as part of our remit. We would shoot the stag and buck that were already at Greenwich and take the new ones up there to replace them. We had to do this because Greenwich has only a small herd in a small paddock and, after three years of breeding, you will have an inbred herd, so you have to keep the bloodline moving.

Basically, it's not easy to shoot a gun in Greenwich, which is one of the main reasons why they're looking at phasing out the cull there. Management's intention is that the deer should be tame and come up and eat a carrot through the wire fencing. They called in our vet, Peter

Green, and he said, 'You'd be better off shooting them all out. I know a place where you can get some really tame deer, who'll feed out of people's hands.' The herd is only twenty in number, and the idea is to get in a vasectomised stag and buck from a farm where they're tame and fed out of a bucket, so they'll be going through all the rituals of rutting, roaring and fighting, but there won't be any end product, i.e. new young. They'll be left alone for ten years to become an ageing herd and then they'll bring in a completely new lot.

Just for the record, Greenwich Park is the oldest of London's deer parks. It predates even Richmond Park. That's why they keep a native herd up there and why they want to keep it going indefinitely. Originally, the deer wandered around the whole area, but over time the deer were moved away from the more popular sections of the park until they were confined to the Wilderness, by the Flower Garden in the south east of the park.

Another reason for the change in policy is that if you work out how much time it takes Tony and me to get to Greenwich, you can see it's just not viable from an economic perspective. I've always said that it might be easier getting to the moon, because it can take us over two hours to drive the fourteen miles across London to get there, and then we have to make our way back to Richmond in the middle of the night with a load of dead deer in tow. Indeed, there was an incident in about 1996 after Dave Smith and I shot fifteen animals at Greenwich and were making our way back home. In those days, the trailer had only two wheels and no spare. At some point in the journey you had to drive through Peckham, which is not the sort of place you'd choose to be stuck in at 2 a.m. if you could help it.

But that is exactly what happened to us, because we got a puncture in one of the trailer wheels bang in the middle of Peckham High Street. It was terrifying, I can tell you. There were gangs all over the place and we thought we were in serious trouble because we had rifles, shotguns, knives and ammo – everything a gang would want. We always bled the animals after we shot them because this helped with the cooling process, which prevented the meat from decaying too fast, but they continued to bleed in the trailer. So underneath the trailer, an enormous pool of blood was running down into the gutter. We were thinking that if a copper pulled up next to us, we would be in deep manure because we had no licences for the guns, as we were Crown-exempt, and we had fifteen dead deer in the trailer. Imagine trying to explain *that* lot away to hard-bitten coppers!

Anyway, I rang our assistant superintendent, who was in a deep sleep, and told him what had happened. He just said, 'OK, see you tomorrow,' and put the phone down on me, leaving us totally alone with no idea how to sort the mess out. We had no AA membership or anything like that, so we had no choice but to drive all the way from Peckham to Richmond with the flat tyre. At one point we had huge showers of sparks coming off the wheel hub as we made our way back down the A3. The hub started out measuring fourteen inches across and it was down to about three inches by the time we got back. We must have been on camera somewhere along the line, but the incredible thing was that we never got pulled over by the police at any point. Now we have a new trailer with four wheels and spares, but that won't be needed under the new system.

On another occasion, I was called out to Greenwich to deal with a stag that had got itself caught up in the wire fencing and couldn't get free. The supervisor, Keith, phoned me at half past three on a Friday afternoon and, as I got my gun and the trailer, I had a feeling that it was going to be one of those days. Anyway, Keith kept ringing me every hour asking where I was and telling me to go a bit faster. I said, 'There's nothing I can do. I'm stuck in traffic and I don't have a blue light.' I eventually arrived just before half past six. I shot the deer and dragged it into the trailer, and it took me another three hours to get home. Six hours for a ten-minute job!

When we were called out to Greenwich (for example on a typical day in January 2016) we'd start at 7 p.m., feed the herd at Richmond, get all our gear on board and set off for Greenwich at 8 p.m. The traffic would be relatively light because we'd leave after the rush hour. We'd arrive at 9 p.m., shoot six animals, bleed them, load them up in the trailer and arrive back at Richmond by 1 a.m., which is not bad going. We'd have to clean the carcasses, check the lymph glands for signs of disease, then wash down, and eventually we'd be finished by

2.40 a.m. I might get back indoors at 3 a.m., so it's a long day, considering we'd do this night shift following a day's normal duties at Richmond.

Every now and then I've been asked if I can help out at other parks, and there have been times when I've gone over to Bushy Park and helped the keeper there to dragnet some of the ponds for a fish survey. As a rule it was nearly always done early in the year, in March or April before fish went to spawn. On one occasion, we did the big Diana Pond, which sits in the middle of the road at Bushy, because they wanted to drain it to carry out refurbishment of the statue and pond base. So all the fish had to come out and be put in holding areas for when it was finished. It was amazing what fish we caught, including bream weighing up to ten pounds, carp up to thirty pounds and tench up to five pounds. It's quite a physical thing to do and it makes for a tiring day. You're up to your chest in cold water most of the time and dragging the net in a particular way so fish don't escape.

Another time, I was called up to London to St James's Park to help Malcolm Kerr, the bird keeper, try to get a sick pelican back into a pen. It was a freezing cold day and I was there from early morning to mid-afternoon, up to my chest in freezing water. Believe me, that makes *everything* shrink. I was numb by the end. This is what I like about this job, though: you never know what you could be doing the next day; there's such variety and nothing mundane or boring.

One of the lodges in Richmond Park has, for many years,

been a royal residence, lived in by Princess Alexandra, who experiences wildlife problems as often as the inhabitants of any other park lodge. I have occasionally been called to her house to solve pest problems and also to give help with injured or poorly animals. The princess is very pro-Richmond Park and very supportive, and wrote me a lovely note once thanking me for my help with a sick fox. My wife Maggie still has the note and, when I had cause to speak to the princess in 2015, her gardener told her that I was going to retire the following year. She said, 'Oh, no. That's a shame. Maybe I can see you before you go.' So I said, 'Maybe. You never know.' We left it at that and I thought no more of it.

A little while later, the rut was on and I received a call from her bodyguard, who was a Met Police firearms officer, telling me that they had a stag up at Thatched House Lodge who was pretty rough. So I went up there and saw this stag lying there looking totally knackered. Princess Alexandra said to me, 'Is he OK?' and I said, 'Yes, he's fine. He's been bonking and fighting all night – he's absolutely worn out.' She found that funny and had a bit of a giggle and I said, 'He's chosen this spot because it's quiet and he's not going to get bothered by anybody.'

Among our many other roles, the Richmond keepers are also civil servants, obliged to keep detailed and accurate records under the Freedom of Information Act. Tony Hatton, my assistant and, as I write, soon to be my successor, was on leave in April 2016, so I used the time to get all the records for 2015 onto the computer. It can take up a whole week. I'm not a whiz on a computer – it's a one-finger job for me – and I remember once pressing PRINT to make one copy, and the machine started printing and wouldn't stop. I panicked and pulled all the leads out of the back of the computer, much to the disgust of the IT unit. It turned out that I'd ordered 250,000 copies.

Throughout the year I keep records for every month: pest control, and what's been shot, in detail. It's like a military operation. I can remember when Tony Banks, the Labour MP and subsequent peer, who was one of the biggest defenders of animal rights, and David Mellor, then a Tory minister and another animal-rights champion, used to ask us for the most detailed information about the last five years: what had been shot; what guns had been used; what methods were used; and so on. Then they would bring it up in Parliament, saying stuff such as, 'Why are all these animals being shot? This isn't fair, that isn't right.' We are really scrutinised here: we're watched from every corner, from the House of Commons to the House of Lords, by the press and the public. So you've really got to be careful what you do, what you say and who you talk to – there are people out there just waiting for you to make a wrong move.

In the days of yore, I didn't attend any meetings – they were held behind closed doors and I didn't know what they were for or who was involved. If they wanted me to know anything they would tell me at three o'clock on a Friday afternoon, an hour before you finished, so you had all weekend to think about it. It was very much 'us and them'. Nowadays we have team meetings, meetings with the Friends of Richmond Park, bird groups – it's endless and I have to attend them all. It's been added to my job description as I've gone along. Also, in my early years in the job I didn't do anything with the media – Brownie did that. I didn't do any filming or TV or radio, or anything with the Friends – Brownie also did those things. Eventually, I was expected to give talks to various groups and to help Simon Richards, the superintendent, when he gave talks.

Back then I didn't have an office, a mobile phone or a filing system, and I didn't record anything. I didn't even record an animal's state of health when it was shot on the cull: things such as its age, sex, bodyweight, fat content, or any problems. I started all of that in the early nineties, and the filing system they use now is down to me. They've got records now going back twenty years on pest control, deer counts, culls, vet reports, licences. Brownie used to deal with all that stuff. He would say, 'You're not paid to get grey hairs. I am.'

So now, as I write this, a lot of my time is spent doing things you wouldn't think I'd be doing. At this time of year, a lot of students ask if they can come and do six months' work experience, working with me and the deer. And I tell them that I don't work with the deer that much. I might do an hour and a half in the morning checking the herd, and that's it. After that I'm looking up a tree for OPM nests eight hours a day. That is if I'm not working on my computer – although 'messing about' might be a better way of putting it, because, as I've said, computers and I do not go well together. They sent me on a computer course once and the woman running it was saying, 'Go to so-and-so' and I said, 'Where? I don't know what you mean.' And she said, 'Just go to it.' So I ended up just hitting button after button and she said, 'What on earth are you up to?' So I replied, 'I told you I didn't know what I was doing.' When it comes to computers I'm a heathen. In fact, I'm still a pounds-shillings-and-pence man.

For me the job has always been its own reward, so I was astonished by the extraordinary event that caught me totally by surprise slap-bang in the middle of the cull in November 2014. I was working nights and I was in the yard on one occasion when Mike Fitt – now officially Michael Fitt OBE, and chairman of the Royal Parks Guild – came to me and said that although he understood that I wasn't one for surprises, he had a big one for me. He told me that I had been awarded the Wildlife Conservation Award given by the Guild to mark twenty-five years working at Richmond Park with the deer. He said that I had to go to Hyde Park on Saturday, 15 November, and be presented with this award, which is given in association with the Deer Study and Resource Centre.

When the big day arrived, Maggie and I donned our best clothes and Jo Scrivener, my line manager, picked us up and took us up to Hyde Park for the presentation, which was made by Colin Buttery, the Royal Parks deputy CEO and director of parks, and Jack Ward of the Deer Study and Wildlife Centre. It's quite nerve-racking when you're sitting there waiting your turn in a room full of people, and everyone who has an award of some kind is going up ahead of you. It turned out that the reason I was last was that it was the most prestigious award of the day.

The award itself was a glass bowl that had been etched with a stag-in-woodland scene, but it was in 3D, so you looked through the bowl and there was one scene on each side and you could line them up. It was an amazingly beautiful work of art – and very expensive, which is why you don't keep it for long. When I had to hand it back, I was given a crystal glass paperweight with my name and the date of my award on it, which was also a beautiful thing to have to mark the occasion.

I have to say that I was gobsmacked by the whole thing. You go through life doing your job, not for a moment thinking about awards of any kind. But to be picked out by the Royal Parks Guild was something special when you think of all the people they could have chosen from the Royal Parks, including all the wonderful volunteers. It showed that someone was sitting there talking about me in a nice way in order to have started the process. It was a truly memorable occasion and I felt proud to have been picked out to mark my time in that way.

CHAPTER TWELVE

The Final Countdown

You have to accept that things change. I started as a keeper; now I'm the Chief Wildlife Officer. The Park will shortly become a charitable trust – a completely new scheme of management. I have lived the life I dreamed of, and it was everything I could have asked for. I have the satisfaction of knowing that I and my colleagues have managed the best herd of wild deer in the country. It's good to leave on a high note.

With my pending retirement date looming over me, there were numerous meetings to attend in October and what seemed like hundreds of emails to deal with. I also activated my pension to start at 1 November. On top of this my wife and I had to move house, and get out of the lodge at Kingston Gate ready for the new man coming. We moved in August to start the process. Mags and I found it very hard. I didn't want to leave it to the last minute, as that would have been even harder. It's felt like being in mourning, and what makes things worse is that I haven't finished with moving things from my old garage and garden yet, so I have to keep going back, which brings up old feelings and memories each time. I have to be out and finished with the house and garden by 31 October and Maggie won't come back to the house with me because it makes her too sad. I found old Snod's grave in the garden, because the staff had been in and cleared an area that covered it. I hadn't seen it in a while and it brought a tear to my eye.

So for the first time in thirty years, I am, as I write this, commuting to work from Walton-on-Thames (welcome to the real world), and I must say it's made me realise that there's a lot to be said for living on site. All I had to do when I lived here was walk out of my back door and I was at work. Suddenly, I was faced with a ten-mile ride before I got here.

Everything has an unreal feeling to it at the moment, with the moving and everything, and I don't think it has really hit me yet that I'm packing up, even with the time fast approaching. I go on leave for two weeks from the middle of September and when I come back on 3 October, I will have twenty-eight days left working as Chief Wildlife Officer for Richmond Park. I have had my last day's shooting in the park, and that was at Isabella Plantation. I don't imagine I will ever fire a gun again.

Over the years I've always tried to get people to come

out on the cull as volunteers to gain experience of what it's like to work with the deer. Some have gone on to work with deer in similar situations to ours at Richmond, but there aren't many parks with red deer; most have only fallow. One or two of the volunteers have subsequently managed to get a position here at Richmond. Kia Handley was one; he came out as a helper for Bushy Park from St James's Park for many years before he got the job here at Richmond. Sadly, he left when the last round of redundancies took place. Normally, when someone gets a job here working with the deer herds, they are here until they either retire or drop dead. It's very rare for a post to come up, and it can be a long time between vacancies for jobs like mine. I'm talking maybe thirty years, like me. So these job are as rare as hen's teeth, as a rule. Thinking about, it by the time my successor, Tony Hatton, retires it will be nearer forty years.

As early as 2007, Ray Brodie, the manager at Bushy Park, phoned me and asked if I had thought of taking on a volunteer for the cull. He suggested Tony Hatton. I said that we should make him an official volunteer just in case he chopped a finger off in the venison house, so we would be covered by our insurance. When Tony first came to work with us he was very quick to learn. He picked things up quickly, and didn't need telling ten times how to do it.

At this point I already knew I would be retiring within the next four or five years, and I sensed then that Tony would make a good replacement. I hoped he would stay on as a volunteer, which he did. I told Tony that it would be a good idea for him to get his DSC1 deerstalking certificate, as this was a minimum requirement to work at Richmond; and I also told him that there would be a post available when I retired. Tony passed the course and went on to build his portfolio ready for his DSC2, which he took and passed when he had finally got a permanent paid job here on 22 February 2012.

After interviewing Tony Hatton, the department allowed him to take my senior position before I left. I didn't doubt for a moment that he would get the job. He has all the credentials and talent to continue after my departure, but replacing him in his previous role will be more difficult. There are very many different aspects to this job, and each one is a vocation in itself. The diverse nature of the work and the demands placed on someone doing this job are the reason why I told the board of governors that it's going to be nigh-on impossible to find someone to replace Tony Hatton when he takes over from me.

From the point of view of someone who likes going out every evening, it's a very unsociable job. You could be working all through the night or on call for seven days, which means no going out with the missus; or, in the case of the 2012 Olympics, you could actually be locked in all week!

I've been called out at all the hours of the clock, whether officially on call or not. It becomes a way of life, and it does take a little getting used to, especially for the wife when she's making plans for the next time you're off and suddenly something happens and you have to cancel them. That's happened hundreds of times for Maggie and me. So it's difficult to find the right person when interviewing for my job because they will need not only particular skills regarding the deer herd, but the right temperament as well to be able to cope with the demands of the job, which involves not just spending more time out in the park than at home with one's partner, but also working in a fish-bowl scenario with everyone looking in. This job is very high-profile, with the public, the press and government ministers often scrutinising your every move – and not many people can take that kind of pressure.

Well, as I write these words, retirement is almost here: time has really flashed past. It's hard to look back and remember how I first came here thirty years ago, full of excitement with all that time ahead of me. I can't believe I won't be able to just go out with the shotgun up Queen's Ride any more or get ready for the cull, working nights and then maybe feeding the herd, which has always been a nice thing to do. The trouble with us humans is that we are creatures of habit and we find things distressing when it's all thrown in the air and our normal routine is changed.

It's also hard to let go of control, and for Tony to take the reins from me while I'm still here. It makes Tony feel awkward as well because of the way it's happening. The trouble for me is that everything that comes in for the attention of the Chief Wildlife Officer goes straight to Tony now, so I'm feeling a little low and surplus to requirements. It can't be helped, as this is how the system works in the civil service. But at this moment in time no one wants me for anything, so I feel at a loose end, which is strange and unsettling.

In contrast to this, everyone suddenly wants to write an article on my thirty years here and my pending retirement. The Friends of Richmond Park did an article for their monthly magazine and the *Ham & Petersham Magazine* did one a week later. So all of a sudden I'm very popular. I really don't know why, as I don't see myself as anything special.

Meanwhile, the yearly intake of cattle arrived, on 5 October to be precise, when Tony happened to have the day off. Four young Belted Galloways from Surrey Wildlife Trust are here for the winter grazing project. It brings back memories for me and it's kind of nice to see them before I go. On the same day a lady brought in a wood pigeon, which had internal problems, so I had to dispatch it – not that I told her that. People don't want to hear the nasty bits.

I had to go with my co-writer, John Karter, to London later that week to meet the publishers of this book, to sort out photos and talk about various elements of the process. It's been a strange experience for me, doing the book. When John first approached me back in November 2015, I had reservations because it felt like laying my life out for everyone to see. But the more I thought about it, the more I realised how good it would be to walk away with a kind of memorial to my time in the park that will cover just about everything I did here and also remind me of all the wonderful people I was lucky enough to work with.

So here I am with twenty-one days left before I go. It irritates me that it took so long to find out what my pension was going to be – typical government-run system. If I dealt with the deer in the way the pension department handled my case, I'd have been out on my ear years ago. They required four months' notice, which they had, but they still weren't able to give me the exact amount I was to receive each month. My worry is that, if they aren't able to sort that out in the four months they've had up to now, how will they handle things in the future?

I have all this to take on board as well as winding down to retirement, so in all my thirty years here this has been my most stressful year. I never dreamed my final months would turn out like this. I thought I would be just riding off into the sunset waving goodbye to everyone. No chance! I'm on call this week for the last time ever, and that's one thing I won't miss. I just hope I don't get any silly callouts, such as a car accident with a deer. I've had my share of these in my time, some of which have been horrific and made the hairs on the back of my neck stand up.

I was hoping it would be a quiet week. I should have known better. There hadn't been any calls for weeks, but typically it then went into overdrive. It's as if everyone, including the deer, knew it was my last time on call. I give it in detail, because it's a very good illustration of the job here.

MONDAY 10 OCTOBER

The antics started when we had to go over to Home Park at Hampton Court to shoot a buck that had a dislocated hip. It had been chased by a dog and must have fallen down a hole, which caused it to pop the hip joint out. We met up with one of the rangers, who was with the woman who owned the dog. The dog hadn't been seen since and it took us a while trying to find the buck, but after two hours it was done.

Then – would you believe it? – I got a call at 8.50 p.m. on the same evening, informing me about two men being chased by a stag in Richmond Park. They had to climb a tree to get away from it, and I said to them that they would have a long night sleeping on a branch. I told them to wait for the animal to walk off and then get down and get out of the park fast, as it had been shut for three hours. As there's no street lighting in the park at night, it's as black as Newgate's knocker.

TUESDAY 11 OCTOBER

The next morning we were looking at the herd to see if everything was OK when a great big master stag appeared with a scrotum the size of a football and testicles so heavy they were hanging down between his knees. He was obviously in trouble and finding it hard to walk, and at this point we knew he had to go, even though we didn't know what was causing the swelling. It could have been a tumour or an infection or something else altogether. We had to get the police out because there were around a dozen photographers all waiting for Tony to shoot this deer and they kept getting in the way trying to get an action picture.

The police turned up and told them no pictures. They said prosecution would follow if they went to print. I shouted at a couple who were still trying it on and explained that it was not a cabaret act and gore watchers should go away – all you're seeing is a beautiful animal being put to death. After what seemed like ages, I drove Tony around and got him in position for a safe shot. Tony managed to get a shot off and killed it in one. It was a great shame because it was one of our best stags. It turned out that the stag had some sort of infection of the bladder and there was also a puncture wound with urine seeping into the stomach cavity and scrotum.

Later I was just about to go home when I got a call for a stag with a broken leg near Pembroke Lodge. I went out there and saw a hind way off in the distance but no stags, so I drove all round the area and couldn't see a stag or a buck anywhere. I decided to leave it until I got a better description of where it was and whether it was definitely a stag. Two hours later I'd driven all the way home, and I was relaxing on the sofa with a coffee when the phone went. I was told that there was a hind near Pembroke Lodge with a broken leg. I thought I must have just passed her by, because they'd told me it was a stag I was looking for, so I decided to leave it until the morning, as it was 5.30 p.m. and by the time I got through the traffic it would be getting dark.

WEDNESDAY 12 OCTOBER

The next morning I got up early so that, as soon as it was light, I'd go out and have a look for this hind. I went out, couldn't find her anywhere, and decided I'd have another look later. At 9.30 I received a call saying there was a stag that didn't look right by Sheen car park. This was my sixth callout since Monday – so much for a quiet last week! I drove down to Sheen and it was just a stag that had been bonking and fighting all night and had worn himself out so was having a nap. The lady who rang in was still there and asked if the stag was OK. I told her he was just exhausted from rutting all night and would be fine.

Coming back, I decided to have another look for the hind with the broken leg but still couldn't find her. I was starting to feel that someone had it in for me. This is exactly how the callout works: you can go weeks with nothing and then for some unknown reason it's a couple of calls every day for a week.

THURSDAY 13 OCTOBER

The next day I was called out for a wasp nest in Roehampton car park on the ground right next to a parking bay. It was a really lively one not far from the cafeteria, so we killed it, but Tony actually did the killing: as I've mentioned, I have to be careful since, due to my allergies, wasp stings can unfortunately be rather too fatal for my liking. This was my seventh callout since Monday.

Then, when I was back in reception at Holly Lodge,

a call came in about the same stag at Sheen, from the same woman as the day before. I explained again that it was fine to leave it alone, but she was worried because it was in the same place as yesterday. I said to her, 'Well, you sleep in the same bed every night, so why can't he?' She rang off thanking me, and we carried on searching for the hind with a suspected broken leg from the day before, but she was nowhere to be seen. That worried me because, if her leg was broken, this was the sort of thing that would make an animal go to ground, wandering off on its own to find a quiet spot where there are no other deer about.

FRIDAY/SATURDAY 14/15 OCTOBER
So now it was the weekend, and I knew that if I was going to get another callout it would be during the next two days, when all the loonies come in after they've done their shopping. Well – surprise, surprise! – I went the whole of Saturday without a call; I couldn't believe it.

SUNDAY 16 OCTOBER
Anyway, the next day I took a call from the lady who thought the stag at Sheen was injured and she insisted she was right and I was wrong. I explained to her in a nice way that after thirty years working with these animals I was more of an authority on the subject than she was and told her that there was definitely nothing wrong with this particular animal. So, finally, she rang off.

MONDAY 17 OCTOBER

Today Tony and I were called out for a stag with a severe limp up by the Royal Ballet School in White Lodge. It took a while to locate him and he was indeed limping, but his leg wasn't broken, as he was putting weight on it, so we reckoned he would be all right. These animals pick up injuries all the time when the rut is on. We had an estates meeting the same day – we actually call it a team meeting – my last one of these ever. It's a chance for us all to catch up with the news, including what's happening with the move to charitable-trust status, and any jobs that need doing across the park. After the meeting finished, I went to get all the remaining items I wanted from the lodge at Kingston for the last time. It still feels like I'm going home every time I go up there, but this was my last chance to see inside the old house as it had been for me and Mags. The next time I'd come by, the new guy would be in it.

TUESDAY 18 OCTOBER

After the previous week's callout finished, with me thinking that was it, I ended up covering a callout for Tony, as he'd taken the day off. I went back up to Pembroke Lodge to see if the stag or hind with the broken leg was there but I couldn't find it. As there hadn't been any more calls about a deer with a busted leg, I assumed it must have been OK.

WEDNESDAY 19 OCTOBER

We started Wednesday at five because we had to zero the rifles for the coming cull. The rifles are all accurate, anyway, because we use them throughout the year, but it's a case of checking them and ensuring that they are spot on for the start of the cull on 7 November. Of course, I won't be around for that. We went out again to check the herd and also to see if the hind or stag with the suspected broken leg was among them, but, again, we couldn't find it, so I felt sure it must have been just a limp and that it had got better. Then we got called out to a dead hind up near Sheen Gate and we were hoping it would be the one with the broken leg, but it wasn't. She'd been dead a while and I was surprised that no one had called it in the previous week, as she was out in the open. We dumped her carcass in Sidmouth Plantation to allow foxes and badgers to eat her rather than let her go to waste. I didn't open her up but she could have been stabbed by an over-randy stag, although it's more likely that she'd swallowed a plastic bag, as she was extremely emaciated.

THURSDAY 20 OCTOBER

We went around the park again today to check the herd, and they were still all going bonkers for the rut. The reason it's going on for so long is probably because it was very hot at the beginning – around 34°C – and stags can't rut in that heat. They would die of heat exhaustion because they have such a layer of fat inside them. So during the early weeks of the rut when they would usually be going for it, they were all under trees trying to keep cool. Now they're making up for lost time.

MONDAY 24 OCTOBER

Tony was training today, so I was on my own. I went round and checked the herd and made sure all the animals were OK. The stags and bucks were still rutting, although they were starting to wind down. The master stags all seemed to be eating nonstop, which is a sign that the rut is coming to an end. I also looked for a small dead deer near White Ash Lodge, where Tony was called out to on Sunday, but neither of us could find it. We didn't know if it was a young deer or an adult fallow female. I also had another look for the stag or hind with a suspected broken leg from last week and couldn't find that, either.

Just six more working days, and we still don't know who the new man taking Tony's old position is going to be or when he'll start, so Tony will be on his own for the first couple of weeks of culling. The dealer came in today and took the carcass of the stag that we shot last week, so at least it didn't die in vain. Once that was out of the way, I was able to wash down the venison house ready for the cull. Strangely, it was a very quiet day, just like yesterday.

I phoned Maggie to find out if the pension people had received my return forms, which they had. Hopefully, that means they will sort out what pension I shall be getting before the end of the week. It was really quiet over the last few days and I was praying that meant it would be like that all week.

TUESDAY 25 OCTOBER

What's that old saying about tempting fate? The next day we went out to check the herd and found a fallow doe with a large tumour hanging from her mouth under the chin. It just shows why you must check the herd every day, because it was the first time we'd noticed this animal with this growth, and yet we check them so religiously.

We decided that the doe needed to be taken out, so we headed back to the yard and got the gun, and Tony drove me back to where it was. Sure enough, it was still in the same place feeding on sweet chestnuts. It was in a difficult position because it was standing on the brow of a slight hill and I had to wait for it to move into a safer position before I shot it. After a few minutes I managed to get a clean shot and what was nice was that all the other animals around it just carried on feeding without batting an eyelid. We got it back to the yard to open it up and see if there were any other tumours growing. There weren't, but we froze it and kept the head for our vet so he could check when he came to see if it was anything contagious.

I was thinking that this would be the last time I'd ever fire a gun and shoot a deer in this job. But, once again, the best-laid schemes – ha-ha! While we were doing this the dead fawn that Tony was called for on Sunday was seen again, with a photo to confirm it this time. However, we still weren't able to find it. This was the third time that we had been out searching for this animal without success, but it was definitely a fallow fawn that was dead out there somewhere.

WEDNESDAY 26 OCTOBER

With four more days left, I was full of butterflies and anxiety with the day of my retirement looming – a mixture of nerves and excitement. Tony was on leave again and making the most of his time while I was there to cover things. I went out and looked at the herd and everything seemed fine. I also had another look for the dead fawn, but still couldn't find it, and I began to think that it wasn't in the area that people were saying it was.

We had to shoot four deer in the last ten days. I couldn't believe it: that made it the busiest two weeks for serious callouts in ages. I had to go to Bisley Rifle Range to collect ammunition for the coming cull and that took up most of the morning, just getting there and back. When I did get back I received two callouts for stags that were supposed to be dying. The first was just knackered from bonking all night and was fast asleep lying prostrate on the ground. The other was also tired but had picked up injuries to the muscles in his ears and couldn't hold them up, making him look like a donkey. I thought he might also have sustained other injuries but couldn't see blood anywhere, so there didn't appear to be anything life threatening Phew! At this rate I'll be glad to retire!

THURSDAY 27 OCTOBER

I have a TV interview lined up at midday with ITV London news, asking me all about my thirty years here. I can't imagine why it's news that I'm retiring – I'm just a nobody. I think they want me to talk about the changes to the park that I've seen in my time. The problem is that you don't know what they are going to ask until they're here.

FRIDAY 28 OCTOBER

Just three days to go now! We went out to destroy a wasp nest up at Pembroke Lodge and I took myself down to Robin Hood Gate to see if the stag that was looking like a donkey yesterday was OK. He wasn't: he had scraped off a large scab, which I'd thought was mud, from his shoulder and it was alive with maggots, so he had to come out.

The trouble was that he was on the other side of Beverley Brook, which meant I would have to get in the brook to get him out after I shot him. I also had to get the police down there with me as there were quite a lot of mums with kids around because it was half-term week. Anyway, I managed to shoot him, and we winched him up onto the bank. His wound was much worse than I'd thought. Again, it was a shame, because he was a really good animal and I wouldn't have been taking him out in the cull in the normal way. He had picked up this injury in the rut – it was just below his shoulder, which is where the antler tips reach. I definitely won't be shooting any more deer in my lifetime. This was the last one ever. That made five: the last time I'd shot as many as this in a week was in the cull back in February.

I had just sorted this all out and washed up when ITV London news turned up ready to start filming. I took them down to the big open Flying Field at Sheen to get some deer behind me while they filmed and asked questions. We had just arrived there and started to film when four men decided they were going to get as close as possible to the herd we were filming and scare them. So in the middle of shooting, I shouted to them to keep back and not get too close – not once but three times. In the end, I had to go over to them and tell them to bugger off before I fetched a copper. I explained that the deer were 'wild', meaning unpredictable.

Then two women were trying the same thing and one of them complained that she didn't want to be on telly! We explained that we weren't filming her: we were filming me. It was turning into a cabaret act. We carried on and ended up filming for two hours for a two-minute scene. The interviewer asked me all sorts of things, some of which involved sensitive issues, and I needed to be super-diplomatic because we try not to upset people. They finished the filming, having got through their hundred questions, and it all went well considering it was mostly done by one man, who did the script, filming and editing to get it ready for TV. So, at 6.20 p.m., I was watching myself on telly and it came across really well. Hopefully, I made some good points about dogs chasing deer, car accidents, people getting too close to the deer themselves and what the animals have to endure from us silly humans.

Following hot on the heels of all this action in the park, I received two messages that had nothing to do with the deer. First of all, Maggie texted me to say that the pension stuff had turned up at long last, so I could get cracking on that. And then I had the biggest surprise of my life: a phone call asking me to attend an audience with Princess Alexandra at Thatched House Lodge, her home in the park, on my last working day, 31 October, at 12.30. I certainly didn't see that one coming.

The staff here have organised a small party for me on Friday, 28 October, so that all of us here at Richmond can have our own little do. I also organised a bigger do at Pembroke Lodge, which Daniel Hearsum, who runs the place, kindly put on for me in the Belvedere Room on my final afternoon. We invited all staff from all the Royal Parks, as I aimed to go out in style. It looks like being some send-off.

I can't help feeling nostalgic about the house at Kingston Gate. You are aware that giving back the house is part of the deal when you take the job, but it still feels very clinical when it happens. After all, it was home. I can remember vividly when we used to put the lights on over the patio at the back of the house and it made the glass patio doors appear like a mirror – you couldn't see inside the house from outside. So we could be sitting on the settee watching TV and badgers would be out there eating the corn we put out for them. You could go up close to them and look right in their eyes because they couldn't see you or smell you. You could almost see them thinking, is there someone in there? You'd get foxes coming right up close, too. They would come night after night – it was better than some of the wildlife programmes you see. The best night I ever had was when there were three badgers, two foxes and a cat, all sitting on my patio next to one another, all – apart from the cat – eating the corn. I've got pictures of them – it was better than anything on the TV. I'd be sitting there watching them and Maggie would be watching *EastEnders* or something!

SATURDAY 29 OCTOBER

With only two days to go I was feeling quite nervous, but didn't know why. Maybe it was because I was venturing into the unknown, never having retired before. Tony and I went out to check the herd and, thank God, we didn't find anything untoward. I started feeling really anxious with the clock ticking away and the staff party looming up. But, when the party actually got started at 1 p.m., I relaxed a bit. Everyone had brought in lovely things to eat and there was enough food for the Eighth Army!

Simon Richards, the superintendent and my manager, made a speech about how he and all the rest were going to miss me. He said they couldn't believe it was happening and couldn't imagine my not being there any more. He presented me with a photo album, which everyone had helped to put together, with pictures I didn't even remember being taken. They went back to when Kia started here with me. It was a great thing to do as I would have had no record of my thirty years here without this album. I was never one for taking pictures. I always left that to others. So, finally, the party was over. Tony dropped me off home.

MONDAY 31 OCTOBER

After thirty years, I can finally ease off and relax a little. I had a lot on throughout the day, but nothing strenuous: the meeting with Princess Alexandra at 12.30; my farewell party at Pembroke Lodge at 4 p.m.; and a few things to finish on the computer – filing, deleting information and printing out material – before the department locked me out for ever.

Tony and I took my last check of the herd to see everything was OK. The animals had definitely finished rutting, as most of the stags were sitting together rather than knocking the hell out of each other, and they were all eating again. So at least I had seen my last working rut. As we went around the park I also had my last chance to see the old lodge at Kingston, where we lived for all those years. I knew I wouldn't be coming back this way for a while and that when I do there will no doubt have been lots of changes to the place for the new man. This all makes me feel sad. I feel as if I were in mourning when I should be feeling happy and excited to retire.

The audience with Princess Alexandra at Thatched House Lodge was particularly special and lifted my spirits. It was a privilege that I don't know of any other retiring employee getting. I was quite nervous, even though I'd met her before, because I didn't know what to expect. There was no precedent and I can't really understand why I'd been picked out for this honour but, despite my nerves, I was really looking forward to it.

I arrived early and waited a while so that I was nearer

to the appointment time before I went into the house. Her gardener, Steve Reed, whom I have known for twenty years or more, met me and I asked him if he had put a word in for me to get this appointment. He said, 'No, she's asked three or four times throughout the year for a chance to meet you before you retire.' I was still really nervous, but I didn't need to be as she came to the door and greeted me and made me feel instantly at ease.

So there I was, sitting on the sofa with Princess Alexandra, in her main lounge, drinking coffee, which she had just poured for me, and making small talk for thirty minutes. She asked me what was I going to do with myself and would I miss the job? She was very interested in what I was going to do after I left the park. It was such an amazing thing to happen to me and really put the icing on the cake for my last day. To be honest, it completely blew me away, and then, just as I was leaving and thanking her and thinking that things couldn't get any better, she presented me with a retirement gift: a leather-bound notepad with fourteen-carat gold corners and her coat of arms in gold on the back. I just couldn't believe it. What an amazing lady. For her to pick me out of all the people who must come and go through her life on a daily basis was just so incredible. I had to keep pinching myself. She really is a princess and I thanked her for her kindness. As I was leaving she said that maybe next time she could meet Mrs Bartram, which again meant I was lost for words – and, believe me, for anyone who knows me that is a rare event.

After I finished my audience with the princess, I went back home to Walton to pick Maggie up and bring her back ready for the four o'clock party at Pembroke Lodge. I was feeling all butterflies in the stomach as I didn't know what anyone had planned. We arrived a bit early and waited outside to meet John Karter to talk about this book, which, between us, we were making great progress with. Daniel Hearsum, who runs Pembroke, had laid on a fabulous spread for me. He's another amazing person, whom I had the luck to meet during my life in the park. The old place soon became pretty crowded and, as the people made their way in, I discovered that they had brought me gifts. For some unknown reason – I can't think why – they must all have believed that I like a drink, because I was given enough booze to sink a ship.

After about an hour of socialising with so many old friends, Simon Richards, the superintendent, called everyone to order and made a speech that made me feel very humble. You don't always know what people think of you until these occasions arrive. I honestly never realised just how much of an effect I'd had on some staff, but I do know what it feels like to have close contact with people and what it's like when they suddenly move on. It leaves a void that nothing seems to fill. So I feel for the ones I'm leaving behind, because it definitely upsets the boat for a while.

Simon presented me with an array of gifts that all the staff had contributed to, including a Japanese maple from Isabella Plantation and a superb pair of binoculars, which

I really wanted. I made a short speech and I can't even remember what I said, except how wonderful it was to see so many people turning out for me, because I'd been worried that it might just be Maggie, me and a huge pile of sandwiches. I was once again lost for words, but I scrambled through and they all cheered me and there were lots of tears among the staff.

I met lots of old members of staff who had retired or had left some years ago and it was really good to see them again and catch up with the latest news. I was particularly pleased to see Kia Handley, my former assistant, and his wife Karen, whom I also hadn't seen for a while. Kia said that he never goes stalking for deer now and hadn't killed one since he left Richmond. In fact, he's not active in that side of things at all these days, because he runs kennels and a cattery in the New Forest area, which are doing really well.

As the evening wore on, the guests started leaving as many of them had to go to work in the morning – and it suddenly hit me that I didn't. I still can't put a finger on any one thing that I'm going to miss more than anything else. All I know is that it's been an absolutely amazing ride for the last thirty years, which made it all the harder to leave. So Mags and I made our way home to our new house. She was crying and we both felt sad.

I decided to go out via Ham Gate instead of my usual route through Kingston Gate, because that would have meant passing by our old lodge again, which would have been a memory too far. It was an exceptionally mild October evening, so I had the car window down. As we swept down the hill from Ham Cross, heading towards my final exit from the park, I heard a sound that symbolised everything about my time there. The roar of a stag echoing eerily through the night rang out, and had me choked up and proud, in equal measure.

Who knows what the next thirty years hold for me? If they are half as good as the last thirty, I won't be doing so badly. I have been an extremely lucky man to have lived this amazing life and to have experienced the very special magic of Richmond Park from the inside. That's something no one can ever take away.

Epilogue

BY TONY HATTON

I'll never forget the first time I met John Bartram – how could I? He's someone who makes an indelible impression on you just by being who he is: a huge presence in every sense. I often say to people who know John that they broke the mould when they made him. To give those who don't know John an idea of what makes him a one-off, he's six foot three and walks around in a pair of Doc Martens, which you could lean backwards in at forty-five degrees and not fall over. He has shoulders that most rugby players would be proud of, a deep, powerful voice and a booming laugh that over the years has become one of the more familiar sounds of Richmond Park.

John is what I would call one of the old-school gamekeepers. He has always said to me that if it's anything to do with fur or feather, it's up to us to deal with it. John has seen many changes during his time in the park, not least in the area of technology. He has gone from having no phone and no computer to pagers and mobiles, emails and lots of computer work and despite initial problems, he has grasped it all remarkably well. I know that there has been the odd time when he has felt like chucking it all out of the office, but I'm sure most people have felt like doing that at some point.

John's talents extend far beyond managing the deer and their wellbeing so skilfully. He can hold his own on TV or in a room full of people asking all sorts of questions to do with wildlife and the park's history. After thirty years of working in the park, there is very little he doesn't know about this unique place that's been his home as well as his working environment. One interviewer was so impressed by his vocal skills, as well as his knowledge, that she said to him he could put Ray Winstone out of a job. That would have made good watching!

John is one of those people who can lay the law down and say what needs to be said and mean it and, once it's been said, you take notice. And a few minutes later he will be making you laugh with one of his stories. Learn from your mistakes and move on – that's his philosophy. He has always said to me, 'Don't hold anything back. If you need to say something, say it, and don't let things fester.' And he's right.

There have been many times when I've been with John and someone's dog has chased a deer. John has had words with the dog owner and, while he is not rude in any way, he is straight-talking. For instance, he will say, 'Put your dog on a lead, it's a chaser. Don't let it off again or I'll have a copper on you.' Some people come back and say they've never done it before, and John will say, 'He [or she] probably has; you've just never seen them do it. Some people are so busy chatting away that they lose track of what their dogs are doing.' John and I are both dog lovers; I have two dogs of my own. But our job is to make sure that the deer and other wildlife in the park are protected at all times. John does that in a firm but fair way, like the professional he is.

To go back to the beginning, my first interest in the Royal Parks began when I was about to leave school; I was fortunate to get a three-year Royal Parks apprenticeship in horticulture back in 1993, working in Richmond Park. Working alongside John and Kia Handley, the two wildlife officers at Richmond, I watched and learned how to clean deer ready to go into the food chain, and also the selection process when culling.

In due course Kia left the Park. At the time there was some uncertainty about the overall job situation at the Royal Parks. It was all a bit of a shock for me and even more so for John. The Royal Parks wanted to replace Kia but the formal process took time. When the position was advertised there were around thirty-five applicants. Fortunately, I was the one offered the job of a lifetime. I know that John was pleased for me and I also think he was happy not to be working on his own any more.

Being a wildlife officer in Richmond Park was totally different from my previous job; in fact it's unlike any other position I can think of, because it's a lifestyle more than a job. Sometimes you're out working all night and other times you're up at the crack of dawn – or even earlier in the summer months – doing pest control. Lots of people ask me about what I do and I always say it's a way of life that I feel lucky to be involved in. It might not be the best-paid job in the world, but working with deer and other wildlife more than makes up for that.

One of the best times for me – and I know it has been for John, too – is when the young deer are being born. John and I have spent many an hour walking through long grass, probably covered in deer ticks, just to find a newborn deer so we can put a tiny tag in its ear. This is done to only a few deer each year to help with ageing them, especially the females. We use a different colour for each year, numbering from one to ten, so if we can get five red and five fallow, it's great. However, this rarely happens: the norm is around two to five a year. They are not easy to find in long bracken or long grass and, if you're lucky enough to find one out in the open, Mum is normally there to kick you into next week if you get too close.

The other time of year that John and I have enjoyed has been winter, when the deer feeding starts. It's an amazing sight to see four hundred deer running towards you in the dark in the lights of the Land Rover. I never get bored of this happening, because it's also a time when you get to see all the animals up close. There was one stag that John named Buster, whose story he recounts in detail in the book. It's worth saying just a few words here about the impact he made on John, and indeed on us all. People often see us as men with guns who have a purely professional attitude to our work, but John is passionate about the deer and all other wildlife. He had a lump his throat when he had to say goodbye to Buster, and you could hear in his voice how distressing it was for him, even though Buster had lived to fourteen years old, which is a good age for a stag.

Working with John over the years has been a great experience in every way. He has passed so much of his knowledge on to me and that stands me in great stead for the future. I'm eternally grateful to him for sharing it with me. He is a true gent as well as a good friend. It was hard at times towards the end for John and me, knowing that he was going to stop at some point soon and I'd be taking over his role. As I've said, working with the park's wildlife is more than a job, it's a way of life, and I know that John found it difficult on some days, such as when we were both out looking at the herd and he would say, 'That's the last rut I will see,' or 'That's the last calf or fawn I'm going to tag.' It was also difficult for me, because it was a partnership that worked so well and was about to end. There were times, though, when John would say that he couldn't wait to go so he could make the most of his love for fishing and birdwatching and also spend more time with his good lady. I know he was really looking forward to enjoying those things without any pressure. And who can blame him?

Looking back, there were some great times taking the mick out of each other – for instance, when we were out doing the pest control in the early summer mornings and John and I would head off in different directions with our shotguns and John would say, 'See you in a bit with a wheelbarrow full.' We would meet up an hour later and I would say, 'Sounds like you were having fun,' after hearing shots ringing out across the park. Then I would see that John had just a crow or squirrel, and he would say, 'I can't hit a barn door this morning. I'd do better throwing the bloody thing at them.' On other days we would both be on good form and hit everything that we saw. Great times – 'hot barrels', as we would say in the shooting world.

There have been many funny moments over the years, as well as some sad ones, especially when we have had to make decisions to end the lives of magnificent animals that are in distress. During the first six months I worked with him I'd never laughed so much in my life. All I can say is that it's been an absolute pleasure to have known John and worked with him – I will miss him a lot. I've told him not to be a stranger, to keep in touch and to come out on the deer feed whenever he wants to, or meet up for breakfast.

It didn't take long for me to realise how big a gap John would leave. The first night of the latest cull felt really strange with him not there. We never had to say to each other, 'Did you do this or that?' It was just done. When you were out culling you both knew what you were looking for, and I knew what John was looking at prior to taking the shot. I really hope he hangs around and doesn't just fall off the edge of the planet, because I know I'll be calling on him when I encounter situations where I need his experience and advice.

As I write these words, I'm looking forward to my new role, because Richmond Park in particular and nature in general are things I'm deeply passionate about. That said, you never stop learning in this line of work, so in one sense it's a step into the unknown. I know there will be huge challenges ahead, because although you grow accustomed to a certain routine with the animals and the seasons, nature has a habit of throwing you a few curveballs and things don't always go to plan, especially when humans enter the picture.

For instance, there was the time when a gang of robbers who'd just held up a local bank tried to escape from the police by scarpering through the park, leaving a trail of guns and banknotes in their wake. Luckily, I wasn't caught up in their escapade, but it just goes to show that anything can happen in this line of work, and I'm well aware that I must expect the unexpected when I step into John's big shoes.

No one can be certain of what lies ahead, but I will do my utmost to ensure that John's legacy is in safe hands; that it is looked after now and in the future, for all to enjoy. Here's to another thirty years celebrating Richmond

Park's stunning natural scenery and, of course, its historic and beloved deer herd.

TONY HATTON
LONDON
OCTOBER 2016